Fighting Against Western Imperialism

ANDRE VLTCHEK

Foreword by Michael Parenti

BADAK MERAH

2014

Fighting Against Western Imperialism

Written by: Andre Vltchek

Foreword by: Michael Parenti

Edited by: Arthur Temungwa

Cover Design and Text Layout by: Rossie Indira

Cover Art by: Milan Kohout

Andre Vltchek's photo by: Alejandro Wagner

First edition, 2014

Published by PT. Badak Merah Semesta, Jakarta

http://badak-merah.weebly.com

email: badak.merah.press@gmail.com

ISBN: 978-602-70058-2-2

BOOKS BY ANDRE VLTCHEK

- On Western Terrorism: From Hiroshima to Drone Warfare. Co-written with Noam Chomsky. (Pluto Books, 2013)

- Oceania: Neocolonialism, Nukes and Bones (Atuanui Press, 2013)

- Point of No Return (Mainstay Press, 2013)

- Indonesia: Archipelago of Fear (Pluto Books, 2012)

- Liberation Lit (Mainstay Press, 2010)

- Exile: Pramoedya Ananta Toer in conversation with Andre Vltchek and Rossie Indira (Haymarket Books, 2006)

- Western Terror: From Potosi to Baghdad (Mainstay Press, 2006)

- The Story of Moana (UNESCO, 2007)

- The Story of Ann (UNESCO, 2009)

- Nalezeny

Andre Vltchek

CONTENTS

FOREWORD

The ultimate goal of U.S. foreign policy is to make the world ever safer and more profitable for international finance capitalism. This is also the goal of the ruling interests in countries other than the United States. The NATO nations and nations in Latin America, Africa, Asia, Eastern Europe, the Middle East, and Central Asia are, for the most part, all dedicated to this same objective and collude with the American plutocrats.

Often overlooked about impoverished Third World nations is the fact that they too are capitalist, which is to say, they too are ruled by elites that work determinedly and faithfully within the parameters of corporate financial accumulation. Such is the case with capitalist Nigeria, capitalist India, capitalist Colombia, capitalist Indonesia, capitalist Honduras, and others too numerous to list. Most of them also are seen in the western mainstream media as "faithful allies," "democracies," "anti-terrorists," purveyors of "humanitarian wars," and other such seemingly virtuous designations.

What really gives them standing with policymakers in Washington is their devotion to wealth and power, their readiness to throw open the land, labor, markets, capital, and natural resources of their countries to the global and regional corporate interests of the world, on terms that are highly favorable to the multi-national investors.

Of course this is not what we are told by our opinion makers and policy makers. Commentators of world affairs in the mainstream corporate owned media---and even others who profess to be further to the left---learn to go only halfway. By that I mean they learn not to cross into forbidden territory, both ideological and informational. They dare not pursue dissident ideas and issues, and they dare not present data that expose the subterranean motives of the global policymakers.

When U.S. policy produces faulty results, criticisms are lodged by mainstream commentators or political leaders, criticisms that are usually filled with false images. We are told that "our" policy abroad is repeatedly confused, timid, inept, bungled, overweening, overextended, deluded, myopic, and burdened by unintended consequences and imperial hubris. The critics are sure they are smarter than the policymakers. In fact, they are deliberately or unknowingly covering up what are the motives that propel U.S. global policy.

The difference between what U.S. citizens think their rulers are doing in the world and what these rulers actually are doing is one of the great propaganda feats of modern history. I made this observation a decade ago and unfortunately, it is as true today as ever. In fact, U.S. interventionist policy around the world is very consistent and very successful. It claims to intervene for humanitarian purposes, rescuing this or that helpless people from the clutches of some wicked aggrandizing dictator or autocratic movement, or defending "U.S. interests" abroad ----interests that are frequently referenced but never really defined in any plausible way. Or we supposedly need to defend our ramparts from terrorists, maniacal foreign leaders, fanatical Muslims, Communists, and other aggressors.

So the United States, with an occasional assist from British, French, or other collusive powers, has intervened in scores of countries using mercenaries, special operation units, paramilitaries, assassination squads, killer drones, well-trained agitators and demonstrators, well-financed elections, NGOs, compliant media, and persistent disruption, capping all this with highly advanced military forces perched on hundreds of bases in over 120 nations, in what is without doubt the largest, most imposing empire in history. All this is allegedly dedicated to keeping American civilization safe and sound.

But in truth, the world that is actually being fashioned by the global plutocracy is not one of liberty and prosperity. The plutocrats really do not want mass populations that are well educated, with a strong sense of entitlement and high expectations about social justice and economic democracy. The plutocrats do not want to deal with competitor nations that pursue self-development, who shun the debt traps of the IMF and the preemptive avarice of multinational corporations.

The plutocrats do not particularly dislike recessions. Recessions in this or that country, including the United States, expand the opportunity to buy up competitors, gain a more monopolistic control over certain markets, break labor unions, depress wages, roll back human services, and leave mass populations less willing or less able to fight back. Wealth feeds off poverty. Upon the deprived multitude feast the privileged few, the 1%.

Now comes Andre Vltchek, an investigative journalist, documentary filmmaker, novelist, and in-depth commentator, a man of many parts who has made his way through the turmoil and torment of numerous nations around the globe, and who throughout his years has spoken truth to power. Unlike mainstream media and even many "progressive" journalists, Vltchek regularly crosses into forbidden ideological territory and comes up with deeply revelatory scripts, insightful scenarios, telling details, and comprehensive analyses.

Consider for instance how he treats the growing use of "regime change," a form of disruptive destabilization going on in a number of countries today, orchestrated by NATO, the CIA, the National Endowment for Democracy and other agencies of the global plutocracy, wreaking havoc from

Ukraine to Thailand to Egypt to Venezuela.

Vltchek notes that the global agenda, led by Washington policymakers and plutocrats, also entails waging subversive agitation against some capitalists rulers themselves, those who commit what I call "economic nationalism." Any leader, movement, or government that tries to use the land, capital, labor, markets, and natural resources of their country for self-development, rather than throwing the people's resources open for plunder, is targeted by the imperialist interests and branded a dangerous autocrat even a psychopath. Once the leader and his movement are demonized, the plutocratic globalists feel they have license to subvert his government and even bomb his people.

Take the case of Thailand. When Thaksin Shinawatra was prime minister, writes Vltchek in the pages ahead, "he attempted to bring in a modern capitalist system to this submissive and deeply scared nation." That itself was already suspect. The global empire prefers submissive and scared nations rather than self-affirming and self-developing ones. Furthermore, Vltchek continues, Shinawatra "housed the poor, introduced an excellent free universal medical care system (much more advanced than anything ever proposed in the United States), free and very advanced primary and secondary education, and other concepts deemed dangerous to the world order, and to the local feudal elites, as well as the army." Thai elites reacted almost immediately against these egalitarian measures. The prime minister "was exiled, barred from returning home to his country, and smeared. There were military coups, mysterious 'alliances,' rumors, and 'secret messages' coming from a 'very high place.' There was outright killing, a real massacre, when the so called 'Red Shirts,' supporters of Mr. Shinawatra (ranging from moderate reformists to Marxists) were butchered by snipers, some shot in their heads."

Vltchek goes further: "One thought kept repeatedly coming to me: many of the places I had been writing about lately are living a very similar reality as Thailand is. Those elected democratically, those progressive in their core, these governments all over the world have been under severe attacks by some armed thugs, bandits, and anti-social elements, even by outright terrorists."

I could go on quoting Vltchek, but his insights await you in the pages ahead. Vltchek is not an armchair observer or cowardly media commentator. He draws compelling firsthand images from his endless travels around the globe. He is unwilling to mute his observations and unwilling to sanitize the tragic and criminal developments he uncovers. This book is a richly informative and engaging collection of writings by a gifted analyst who deserves a vast audience.

———————

Michael Parenti
Author of The Face of Imperialism (2011) and
Waiting for Yesterday (an ethnic memoir, 2013).

Andre Vltchek

INTRODUCTION

Why are the streets of New York, Washington D.C., London and Paris so orderly, so quiet?

Are we – opposition investigative journalists, philosophers and documentary filmmakers – doing such a terrible job? Are we not providing the North American and European public with enough information, enough proof about the monstrous state of the world? Enough so they – the citizens of the Empire – finally get thoroughly pissed off, detach their backsides from their couches and chairs, and flood the capitals and business centers with their bodies, demanding change, demanding the end to atrocities that are being committed all over the world... the end of this imperialist and neo-con madness?

Are we failing, squarely and patently, to give examples and proof of the pain this world is suffering because of the bestiality of market fundamentalism, because of unchecked neocolonialism and shameless Western supremacy? Are we not providing enough stories and images, enough footage, to convince the citizens of the countries that are ruling the world, that something has gone awfully wrong?

The answer is yes, and also, no.

Yes – we work relentlessly and, frankly; we work well... we

fight well, day and night, often 25/8 (overtime, 24/7), forgetting about exhaustion, personal life, even our health and danger.

On the side of reason and decency, on the side of the resistance against the oppressive and murderous Empire, are the brightest minds of this world.

There are great philosophers and thinkers like Eduardo Galeano, Alain Badiou, Naomi Klein, Arundhati Roy, and Noam Chomsky, who clearly and precisely define and critique the essential concepts that govern the world.

There are brave international lawyers like Christopher Black, and celebrated economists, including the Nobel Prize laureate, Joseph Stiglitz.

Almost all the great writers are part of the resistance, including those – the greatest ones – who have just recently departed: Jose Saramago, Gabriel Garcia Marquez and Harold Pinter.

And there are, of course, investigative journalists, on all the continents, those who are risking their lives, often with no institutional support, working mostly against all the odds.

***

So Yes – we are providing plenty of information, plenty of images, plenty of proof, that the world is in flames, that tens of millions are dying, that true democracy everywhere is being raped and the natural resources of poor countries are being plundered, so that Western capitalism can flourish.

But No – we are not managing to improve the world. All those tremendous efforts are failing to ignite even those few millions of educated and concerned citizens in the West, to organize and rebel, to demand the end of the global imperialist onslaught.

All the information mentioned above, about the horrors of imperialism and market fundamentalism, is easily available on-line, "just one click away", to use corporate language.

But nothing is happening. The majority of Europeans and North Americans appear to be thoroughly apathetic towards the state of the world. They keep stuffing themselves on cheap, subsidized food; they amusing themselves with the latest gadgets (including smart phones, sated with Coltan taken from the Democratic Republic of Congo, where some ten million people have died since 1995). They keep voting in those right-wing governments and they believe, increasingly and blindly, that their societies are an inspiration to the rest of the world as the sole examples of democracy and freedom.

The citizens of the Western Empire are actually so lethargic and indoctrinated, that even when billions are stolen from them (not just from the people in their colonies), when banks get bailed-out after their speculative orgies, or after so-called elections get fully subsidized and manipulated by the corporate mafia, they do nothing; absolute nothing!

Go to a pub in the UK or Germany, and 'everybody knows everything'. You will hear it repeatedly: 'politicians are swine', 'corporations are controlling elections'. If you stay long enough, after several pints of beer someone will perhaps slam his fist on the table: "We need revolution!" Then everybody agrees and they all go home... and the next day – nothing.

'Occupy Wall Street' activists got roughed up by the police... And nothing. Everybody goes home. And shouts at the television.

***

Is there still anything that will outrage people to the point that 'they would actually not go home'? That they would stay on those bloody streets, build barricades and fight, as they did in the past, even as recently as in 1968?

How many millions have to die in the Western colonies, before the people in Europe and North America pay attention, recognize the massacres and admit that they are actually citizens of a fascist empire, and that it is their moral obligation to fight it and dissolve it? Is 10 million in the DRC not enough? Is one coup after another that the West openly orchestrates, not a sufficient eye opener?

***

As President Obama pointed out, honestly, on May 28 2014, at West Point, NY:

"In Egypt, we acknowledge that our relationship is anchored in security interests – from the peace treaty with Israel, to shared efforts against violent extremism. So we have not cut off cooperation with the new government."

Or, to put this into perspective, to quote The Economist (May 24, 2014):

"Prodded by a fawning reporter to reveal the extent of American plotting in support of the Muslim Brotherhood, a theory much harped on by Egypt's xenophobic post-coup media, Mr Sisi disarmingly confessed that the only interference he could recall was when the American ambassador requested that last year's coup should be delayed for a day."

But it is not just in Egypt, although Egypt as well… It is one coup after another, these days, all over the world. Coups financed and arranged by the US and Europe… and all those countries ruined, bombed or run to the ground. We can see them clearly, as we are shown images (with twisted commentaries) every day: from Egypt to Ukraine to Thailand. Destroyed Libya and crippled Syria. Bleeding Bahrain. Countless attempted coups against any progressive Latin American governments. A multitude of African nations terrorized by the West – from Mali to Somalia, to DRC to Uganda.

France is increasingly behaving like a bandit nation. Entire regions covered by blood and pus, governed by gangsters who are maintained and armed by the Empire, decades after many great leaders had been either assassinated or shamelessly overthrown.

There is plenty of evidence and information about all that I am talking about.

If the West cannot murder or overthrow a government in a powerful country, it risks lives in its client states: I have just left Manila, Philippines, where two leading academics, Eduard and Teresa Tadem, explained to me how the United States is pitching Southeast Asian nations against China; their historic and natural ally.

The country's press is servile and so, all the terror of European colonialism and of the US extermination campaign against the Philippine people has been miraculously forgotten. Propaganda works. China is the villain! Western propaganda is brilliant, professional, and deadly. Nobody knows anything about the disputed islands; nobody studies history or legal documents. But China is simply wrong. It must be wrong, because that is what has been repeated on television and in the newspapers every day, for years.

The West is antagonizing China, relentlessly, while spreading anti-Chinese propaganda everywhere, totally discounting the country's enormous achievements and the fact that it is undergoing some profound socialist reforms, related to medical care, education, housing, arts and public transportation, just to mention a few. Of course, any notion that China is a successful socialist state has to be destroyed (it either has to be a failure, or it has to be portrayed as capitalist).

These provocations, many of them of a military nature, are now using the old regional imperialist power, Japan (and its extreme right-wing Prime Minister), which is in sudden need of 'protection'. Needless to say, all this can easily lead to WWIII.

The same provocations are taking place against Russia – against Latin America…and Zimbabwe, Iran, Eritrea – basically against any country that is unwilling to succumb to intimidation, or to sacrifice its own people and lick the boots of the Empire.

And the Western public is blind and deaf. Or it pretends that it does not know and does not see.

There are two possibilities why: either, as I wrote in my earlier analyses (including "The Indoctrinated West"), the

Western public is totally lost and overrun by corporate propaganda (it appears to be the most ignorant and misinformed public I have encountered anywhere in the world). Or it simply pretends to be like that, because the status quo suits its interests – it can take advantage of the looting and plundering done by its governments and companies, while pretending that it is still morally superior to the rest of the world... with hardly any feeling of guilt.

***

We write and write, film and talk... Huge accusations are made, crimes confirmed... But again: nothing happens!

The most disturbing fact is that no revelation, no discovery of crimes committed by Western governments and companies is upsetting enough, or monstrous enough, for the men and women of the Empire, to demand the immediate resignations of their governments, or of the changing of their entire political and economic system.

Genocides are apparently not sufficient reasons to demand the disbanding of the regime.

The overt nature of thieving, the perverse, nihilist economic and social system controlled by kleptocrats, provokes no major revolutionary actions, no nation-wide rebellions. Even demonstrations are diminishing in size. If there are actually any demonstrations, they tend to be of a pathetic caliber – for higher wages, for instance, but hardly ever for ideological reasons.

How often, do we see huge protests in Europe, against the plundering and murdering of people in Africa or Asia... or against, say, the "French New Wave" of imperialism? Or against the monstrous AFRICOM that sits right in the middle of Europe – in the city of Stuttgart? That monstrosity is, according to its own words: 'responsible for U.S. military operations and military relations with 53 African nations – an area of responsibility (AOR) covering all of Africa except Egypt', and it is crammed into the Kelley Barracks, on the outskirts of the city of Stuttgart... which in turn produces all those Mercedes and Porsche cars for the corrupt elites and their children, all over the world.

Nobody protests and nobody gives a damn. I have witnessed some demonstrations against a new train station in Stuttgart, because a few trees had to be cut down in order to build a new terminal... there were demonstrations against the destruction of the 'historic character of the station', but I never saw any substantial demonstration against AFRICOM or against the destruction of millions of lives, all over the world, by German companies.

Europeans (and North Americans) appear to be totally 'bullet-proof' against any information that could lead to making them feel co-responsible for the plunder and devastation that their Empire is and has been spreading, for years, decades, even centuries, all over the world.

As there is hardly any retrospective feeling of guilt, outrage and horror for colonizing, raping and looting basically the entire planet (including North America, as the killing of native people there was done mainly by the first and second generation of European migrants), there seems to be very little chance that Westerners will now rise and demand an end to the terror they are responsible for having imposed on Africa, Asia, Middle East, Latin America, including Oceania.

Great proof was provided by John Perkins when he wrote, "Confession of an Economic Hit Man", a book that made it to The New York Times bestseller list. Several million copies were sold in various languages, and... nothing!

I met John at the studios of INN in New York City. He was interviewed about 'Confession' and I was interviewed about my documentary film "Terlena – Breaking of a Nation", which was about the insanity and brutality of the Indonesian regime after the US-sponsored coup of 1965/66.

We exchanged notes. In his book, John wrote a first-hand account about his former activities and duties. Working for the State Department, he used money, sex and alcohol to corrupt governments in places such as Ecuador and Indonesia, so they would accept totally useless and unserviceable loans that would disappear into the deep pockets of the elites, and bring nothing else other than total misery to the poor and middle classes. Why? The answer was simple: Because indebted countries were easier to control.

Of course, in any normal country or society, such a revelation would bring down the government along with the entire political and economic system. There can be no question that this is the pinnacle of 'immorality', and a system that produces this kind of global scenarios, should never even be trusted with governing, its own nation.

But nothing has happened in the United States. As far as I am concerned, there were no major demonstrations triggered by Perkins' book.

In Budapest, much, much less, triggered the 'uprising' of 1956 – an uprising that was partially provoked by the West (including by the propaganda arm of the US government – 'Radio Free Europe'), and later glorified as the fight against Soviet rule in Eastern Europe.

An extremely uncomfortable but definitely honest conclusion is that the citizens of the West are incapable of, or unwilling to fight and defend the lives of those whom their Empire destroys. They cannot be trusted, anymore. They have failed for centuries.

People all over the planet have waited and hoped that opposition will come from within the Empire.

It took China to rise up, in order to stop military attacks against its territory. Russia had to regain its strength and to get rid of all the horrible rot that was turning the nation into yet another "client state" of Washington – from naïve nitwits like Gorbachev to the tyrant and alcoholic, Yeltsin. And it took Latin America several decades of fights and revolutions, and hundreds of thousands of martyrs, to finally forge a huge united front against the colonialists and fascists from the North.

***

But what I want to ask today is: how, if until now, nothing has worked... how do we deal with the Western public; how do we address it?

Does it really make any sense to speak to them, to appeal to them, even after they had shown such ignorance, such vicious stupidity, indifference and servility?

Would bombarding them – Europeans and North Americans – with facts change anything?

If I show them what they have done in Eastern and Central Africa, would they rebel? We know the answer, and it is: no, they will not.

If we tell them what they are doing to Ukraine, would they demand that all aid to those gangsters who are now holding power there (including that 'newly elected President'), stops? Definitely not! For most of them, Ukraine is nothing else other than a bit of titillating news they watch in the evening, while stuffing themselves at their dining tables.

Most of them do not pay attention. They do not know and do not want to know... all the while pretending that they are the best-informed part of the world. That's not good enough for the citizens of the countries that are ruining the world.

I do believe in collective guilt and collective responsibility. The more I see of European culture, its evasiveness and deception; the more I believe, the more I am convinced that it has to be insisted on. They don't like it, naturally. Tell them about collective guilt and they turn against you like a mad bunch of pit bulls... for very logical reasons. To be a citizen of the continent that is guilty of the destruction of the planet, for many long centuries, is not a joke; it is quite a serious responsibility, and burden... Tell a rapist that he is a rapist, and he breaks your skull. Tell gangster that he is a gangster and just wait and see what will happen.

***

So what to do? Should we stop writing? Of course not!

There are decent people out there, too. Our readers... For them, and only for them, we write, we labor and risk our lives.

But how and where do we go from here? What is the strategy?

Frankly, I think that facts wrapped in academic writing can change nothing. Absolutely nothing. They can get someone a tenure or even put things 'on the record', but do not expect that those facts and 'records' could trigger a revolution, real change.

As it is, all the crimes of the Empire are already very well documented. Information can be effortlessly accessed, read and understood. So we can very easily conclude that pure facts are not moving anyone, anymore. Otherwise the whole field, the entire situation would be quite different by now.

'Facts' are now effectively used only against Communist countries and parties by the elaborate and pointed Western propaganda machine, and here we are talking about inflated, exaggerated and twisted 'facts'. They are repeated thousands of times, over and over again, and as in Nazi Germany, they became truth: the globally accepted truth.

But even many left-wing intellectuals, as Badiou confirms, are readily accepting those re-invented and re-conditioned 'facts', although they also claim that they also know that the individuals and companies that are spreading them, have a clear interest in perverting the truth through their corporate media and corporate universities, which makes it all one great contradiction.

Working in all those places that are used as examples, as the 'proof of evilness of Communism', I can testify that the 'facts' presented by the Western propaganda apparatus, range from being inflated, to being absolute lies. That goes for Ukraine (including the 'famine' of the 1930's), Cambodia, and North Korea, the Soviet Union's gulags, the Chinese famine and the Cultural Revolution. Half-truth is, as we know, much more dangerous than outright falsehood.

To contradict those fabrications in one or two publications is pointless. It would be just you, and couple of those who know what you know, and are ready to risk everything and go public with it, against those hundreds of thousands repetitions and reprinted falsehoods, against their trolls, even their establishment academia and press. You cannot win.

I tried with the Rwanda genocide: that outright complex lie, manufactured by Western propaganda, which I have perfectly documented. You cannot win – trust me, even if you have unlimited evidence.

Then what else?

Would the books of confessions of those Western apparatchiks help? If Perkins failed, who can do better?

Investigative journalism? The same as academic writing: it does not seem to move anybody, anymore. Definitely not to 'move them to action'…

I personally went through hell, through fire, and few of those sniper attacks, through death sentences and through being tortured, even being "disappeared" once… all this, in order to inform, to fire-up people, to outrage them, to piss them off. So they do their part and help to stop the genocides that I witnessed all over the world. But did I change much? Did I manage to stop Western invasions or to prevent their 'coups'? I don't think so…

***

I am giving up on journalism and on academic writing. I actually gave up on them, totally, at least two years ago.

I am back to where it all used to be, before corporate journalism. I am a left-wing writer and a filmmaker. I do not hide it; do not lie. That is what I am, and proud of it. Tradition is great, and I am honored by our tradition, too: from Hemingway and Orwell, to Ryszard Kapuściński and Wilfred Burchett!

I go to war zones to fight for revolution, to be in the resistance against imperialism. I don't go there to 'write objective articles' (that stuff is total lunacy, 'objective reports'). Tripods, computers, cameras, recorders – all of them are my weapons; our weapons.

In many of the places where I go, people are dying. Many of them are dying. Women are being ravished, villages and cities bombed and burned.

All of us, including Hemingway, Orwell and Burchett were, of course, artists and poets. And this is how they wrote.

And this is the conclusion to which I am now arriving:

When in war, when defending revolutions, when fighting imperialism: one has to be, and to write as a poet... Each report has to be part of a great novel which will be written in the future, or which is being written right there, as one prepares his or her reports. Otherwise it is all shit, and will touch nobody and change nothing.

This is where our only advantage is, against those corporate whores: we are human and alive and we have a heart that is on the left and blood that is red, and all that we do is because we love this world passionately... we love this humanity... and we fight and are ready to die for it.

Every report should have at least one poem hidden inside it. It has to touch. It has to offer warmth and relief, and it has to outrage and lead people onto the barricades.

We have to learn how to write like that, again. Otherwise everything is really lost!

And then, instead of recycling as those corporate scribes and academia do, we have to listen to the people, and not to the establishment, not to each other.

The greatest Latin American storyteller, Eduardo Galeano, once told me, deep in the wilderness of his old café in Montevideo: "Why do I write like this? Because I am a passionate listener."

Yes. Human stories are subversive, honest and mostly revolutionary. If a writer truly listens to the people, he knows what to write and how. And he knows how to fight for the people and how to defend them, instead of serving corporations.

I listen, too. Wherever I go, I listen. I don't watch television. Instead I listen to stories.

I have asked many questions today. I'm not sure I know the answers:

How to be effective? How to move people? How to inspire them, so they join the struggle for a better world, even if it were against their own immediate interests and privileges?

What I write is for you, my readers. I do not write in order to hear myself speak, but to convey to you what others have said, as well as how others are suffering and dreaming.

To quote a great poem and song by the Chilean artist, Violeta Parra:

Thanks to life, which has given me so much
It gave me laughter and it gave me longing
With them I distinguish happiness and pain
The two materials from which my songs are formed
And your song, as well, which is the same song
And everyone's song, which is my very song

I want you to talk to me, my readers. I have written so much; you have read what I have written, patiently. Now write to me. I want to listen. How do we go forward? You and I, together... What touches you? What makes you cry? What would make you rise up and struggle for a better world? How do we coordinate our steps and walk forward, together?

How do we fight against fascism, together?

***

This book compiles ten modified essays that were written during just a few months of the onslaught of the Western imperialism all over the world. Counterpunch, RT, Global Research and some other periodicals published my work on almost a weekly basis.

I travelled to Egypt, Ukraine, North Korea, China, Thailand, Venezuela and many other countries, searching for parallels, similarities; comparing scenarios.

I tried to grasp, and then to explain, how the Empire really works, how it selects its targets, which countries it decides to destroy and why? I studied the 'opposition movements' manufactured by Washington and London, and how they get implanted in so many different parts of the world; basically wherever people and their governments still dare to insist on defending their own national interests and choosing their own political as well as economic systems.

I believe that this book is very urgent. Because I trust that the Empire has already reached the point of no return and is now pushing our humanity to a total catastrophe. It is obvious that it is ready to destroy, to bulldoze everything that stands in its path to the total control of our planet. Millions of human lives matter little. The possibility of WWIII is of no concern to the market fundamentalists and their political lackeys.

I wrote these essays and compiled this book as a warning. Frankly, I am terrified by what I have been witnessing allover the world. Western fascism, in its ugliest shape imaginable, is suddenly back. It is gangrenous but still capable of triggering an enormous global genocide. Shockingly it appears to be marching everywhere, almost unopposed.

There is still some time for the disaster to be stopped, prevented. Not much time, but some. And there are still some countries that are ready to defend the world and the human race.

As always, there is some hope. But hope does not bloom from idleness, cowardice and spinelessness. Hope has to be nourished. It will be nourished. It will be fought for!

1

IMPERIALISM IS NOW MURDERING STORIES

Nothing frightens fascism and its older brother imperialism more than real people and their honest stories.

It is because ordinary stories of ordinary people are so genuine and so accurately reflect authentic human fears, desires and dreams that the ideologues and propagandists of the Western regime, which is supported by unnatural hyper-pseudo-reality, feel, for their survival, that it is essential to annihilate those stories, to wipe them from the surface of earth, even to erase them from our memories.

Real human feelings get in the way; they still resist, block the path to the total commercialization of life and the full implementation of the perverse concepts introduced by the Empire. Such resistance is described and glorified in real stories, making them 'extremely dangerous' and potentially fatal to the regime.

Human nature is fundamentally optimistic and kind; it is mostly evenhanded and sharing. If it is not grossly manipulated, fooled, even conned; it generally puts the life of others well above cold profit. It is disposed to be compassionate, forgiving and accepting. It is not perfect, far from it, but as the French philosopher and writer Albert Camus declared at the end of his brilliant novel "The Plague": "there is more to admire than to despise in humans".

That is all very bad news for market fundamentalism and for the masters of the world. They need to ensure that the majority of the human race consists of greedy individuals, aggressive people, people who do not think or feel but consume, and, if they do think, about how to amass more, consume more; definitely not about how to build a decent and egalitarian society.

* * *

Each human life is made up of stories, of true and sincere stories. Some stories are 'common' and can occur, with certain variations, in any part of the world.

A boy meets a girl, and their love is 'forbidden', because they belong to a different class, ethnicity, or religion. They fight for their future together, against all oppressive customs and taboos, and they win or they fall. But after their epic struggle for happiness, their village, or their clan, will never be the same.

A son of rich man walks down the road in a miserable village, right near his mansion. He meets an old man or a woman. They sit for a while and talk.

Poor peasant conveys a message to a young feudal lord. Later this provokes questions, doubts and thoughts; he studies. One decade later he joins the revolution, to overthrow his own class. Almost all men and women of the revolution lived through that moment when they were told the truth on some dusty country road: Che, Lenin, Engels, Marx, Mao, Fidel, Chavez.

Some stories are extremely unique and powerful:

As documented in a great book written by Ron Ridenour "Backfire", several Cuban men and women are approached by the CIA and asked to destroy their own country, to kill innocent people, to cause explosions on board civilian airliners in the middle of the flight, to assassinate Cuban leaders, to poison humans and crops with chemicals. They accept; they take money. Then they immediately join the Cuban intelligence and for years work as 'double agents', to protect, to save their beloved Cuba. There is not one moment of hesitation. Fatherland is not some commodity; it is not for sale! The Personal lives of some of them are ruined in the process. They keep no money for themselves. They give their entire CIA pay to their country, to buy medicine and other necessities. They feed North Americans with false information. Eventually the story is made public. They save Cuba.

Such are the great stories of decency, of courage, of progress.

"My life is my story", once uttered a brilliant German film director, Wim Wenders. The identity of each person, no matter how rich or poor, educated or simple, consists of memories and dreams, and of extremely complex and fascinating webs of stories.

Most 'real' stories are wise, and they contain unmistakable sparks of humanism. Many of them are also aiming at something that we are all secretly longing for from the bottom of our hearts: something very positive, warm, compassionate and tender. They are yearning for good conclusions, not for some toxic and pinkish Disney or Hollywood-style 'happy ending', but for solid, just, and decent finales.

That is exactly why real stories' are becoming targets of hit men hired by the Empire.

In order to plunder unopposed, to control, and to manipulate, the Western Empire assumed that it has to give legitimacy to its own acts of terror. Those acts have to be elevated to the highest moral ground.

To do so, traditional logical and philosophical thinking has to be decomposed, then 'new thinking' introduced. A thoroughly new breed of stories must emerge, and even how stories are told must change.

Some would ask: 'How could crime be packaged as

altruism'?

It can, of course, in those societies that perceive 'reality' after getting stoned on huge daily doses of advertisement and propaganda, two sides of the same coin, two synonyms of lie and deception.

In order for the brutal Empire to pose and to be considered as the savior of the world, first the analytical thinking of people has to be damaged, their ability to think has to be sharply reduced. The stories they are told have to become 'light', 'entertaining', extremely far from the reality.

The human spirit has to be broken, human nature reshaped.

Then all that is real and decent and pure in people has to be dragged through a muddy and nontransparent bath of nihilism. Things that used to be sacred have to be spat on, optimism humiliated, and ordinary kindness and warmth killed.

Instead, substitutes have to be injected, if needed, by force.

It is because the acts of imperialism, like constant plunder and the commodification of life itself, are grotesquely unnatural occurrences; they are morbid and pathological. And the only way they can be accepted is if the reality is canceled, and then substituted by a 'new', gruesome and irrational pseudo-reality.

* * *

If in thousands of brainless Hollywood films, millions of people continuously vanish, victims of mutants, robots, terrorists, giant insects or microorganisms invading the earth, then the public becomes hardened, and 'well prepared for the worst'. Compared to those horrors of pseudo-reality, the real agony of millions of men, women and children in places like Iraq, Libya or Afghanistan appear to be quite insignificant.

"Their children get cancer from depleted uranium coming from our bombs, or they get simply torn to pieces... well, guess what: our children are eaten by monstrous tarantulas or murdered by Arab terrorists..." Those words are not pronounced, of course. The monologue takes place in the subconscious realm.

If a false giant shark begins stuffing itself with the actors depicting defenseless swimmers on a picture-perfect resort beach, such fictitious terror shocks more viewers and at much greater extend than some real violence unleashed against the prisoners at the US torture and detention centers like those at Abu Graib or Guantanamo.

Pseudo-reality is designed to dwarf reality.

Using the same concept, the viewers tend to feel much greater shock when California keeps falling off the cliff to Pacific Ocean, in one of those disaster movies, than when they read about dozens of real and decent governments all over the world being overthrown by the Empire for simply being 'too decent', even when millions of real people perish in the process.

Psychologically, for many people there is no border between reality and pseudo-reality, anymore. Consumers of blockbuster movies and the mass media were made immune to the real terror the Empire is spreading all over the world, because they have already seen 'much more frightening' stuff beaming from the box.

Simultaneously, indoctrination gets encoded permanently in people's brains; they cannot make the distinction, anymore, between some outright BBC propaganda against China or Cuba and the reality they encounter when they visit those two countries.

Some now judge the world and make political and other decisions strictly based on that hybrid of reality and pseudo-reality: "Chinese murdered brutally several thousands of people when they torpedoed some fictional ship, as we witnessed in the latest Hollywood blockbuster, therefore we have to finance their 'opposition' and send our battle ships to East China Sea, to deter the potential expansion plotted by Beijing."

And if our film studios and pop writers keep demonizing Chinese people, South Americans, Russians, Arabs, Iranians, North Koreans and many others, the imaginary threat, in some very twisted but well calculated and effective way, suddenly begins to justify real and countless aggressions by the military forces of the Empire.

* * *

The Empire that consists of Western fascist regimes that call themselves 'democratic' and 'free', have already murdered several hundreds of millions of human beings on all continents. They dropped mountains of bombs and biological weapons on countless countries; they have experimented on people, and overthrew most of the governments that were determined to serve their own people. They murdered Presidents and trained gangsters, whom they elevated to the ranks of top military brass, as happened in Indonesia, Chile, Egypt, El Salvador and in many other places. These gangster-soldiers were then given training, on Western military bases, in the 'art' of interrogation, torture and punitive rape, as well as 'disappearance' of the opposition.

No other system spilled more blood; no other system plundered more resources and enslaved more people, than the one we are told to describe by lofty and benign terms like 'Western parliamentary democracy' or 'Western constitutional monarchy'.

But the writers of 'new stories' and manufacturers of pseudo-reality do their absolute best to block this line of thinking. There is no discussion about the fact that the world is now fully enslaved by Western neo-colonialism, that it is controlled and oppressed to the greatest possible degree.

The past is already fully changed and re-written, with collaborators coming from the ranks of both academia and so called 'liberal' and 'creative elites'. Grotesque lies are thousands of times repeated and therefore, as was suggested by the chief ideologist of Nazi Germany, they became truth. As Joseph Goebbels so correctly observed, many decades ago: "If you repeat a lie often enough, it becomes the truth."

The lies are retold about China, the Soviet Union, Latin America, about Western colonialism, and neo-colonialism, the

Cold War, Afghanistan, and so many other essential places and events. Almost all related stories, except those that were pre-selected, approved, and useful for the propaganda, had been successfully eradicated, muted, or at least ridiculed.

Inside the Empire itself, almost nobody is protesting, except when it comes to demands for higher wages and better benefits. The Western masses became the most complacent, uncritical group of people anywhere in the world. It is obvious from the art they are producing and consuming, from their political affiliations, from their aspirations.

An amazing paradox has developed, without being noticed or commented on: 'the system, which has been professing both individual choice and extreme self-centeredness, actually managed to reduce a substantial part of the human race to an obedient, thoughtless, submissive, and frightened mass of uniformed beings convinced about their own superiority.

The individuality of people almost entirely vanished. Their identity is now closely linked and fully dependent on the manufactured identity of television stars, pop musicians and footballers.

* * *

It is logical and essential that the Empire tries to make sure that the real stories get discredited, destroyed, wiped out from the face of the earth; in order to prevent lapses, in order to make sure that human brains stop doubting and accept what they are being served.

Even the closest historic allies of real stories have been kidnapped, corrupted, and forced against them: books, films, music, and theatres, even fairytales.

But to the dismay of their tormentors, while in terrible pain, abandoned and endlessly sad, the stories do not seem to yield. It is because they are brave and proud, as human beings essentially are, and they know that so much depends on them – they are holding one of the last lines of defense against the capitalist genocide, against commercialization of life itself,

7

against the attempt to exterminate human species as we know it.

As a storyteller I know all this, because they, the stories, are always talking to me. I also know that we will hold that imaginary defense line until the very end, together, come what way, with others who are still capable of thinking and hoping, and dreaming.

We will never cease telling the stories, real stories, because that is what human beings have been doing for centuries and millennia; telling stories, listening, learning, reading, moving forward, reluctantly, stumbling but moving nevertheless. We will be holding the line of defense against cultural fascism, because to succumb would simply be like betraying everything that makes life worth living.

For centuries and millennia people were dreaming about justice and kindness, they were fighting for better world where everyone has roof over the head, and food, free education and medical care, where there is no fear and no danger coming from beastly and greedy usurpers.

The 'real' stories were carrying such dreams, in their core.

Several years ago I sat in an old Café Brasilero in Montevideo, Uruguay, with one of the greatest Latin American writers, Eduardo Galeano, a man who wrote some of the most magical and powerful stories in the 20th century.

Before we parted, he said:

"I am a hunter of stories; I listen to the stories, then I give this back to the people after putting the stories through a creative process. My position is always that in order not to be mute, one shouldn't be deaf. One has to be able to listen in order to speak. I am a passionate listener. I listen to reality. Reality is a magic lady, sometimes very mysterious. To me she is very passionate. She is real not only when she is awake, walking down the streets, but also at night when she is dreaming or when she is having nightmares. When I am writing, I am always paying tribute to her – to that lady called Reality. I am trying not to fail her."

If the regime decides to starve us, real storytellers, we will, as in the marvelous story of Gabriel Garcia Marquez, "No One Writes To the Colonel", rather "eat shit", than to betray that magic lady called Reality. The stories, the reality is not for sale, as the truth itself is not for sale.

* * *

At the last page of an old copy of the novel "River of Fire", written by Qurratulain Hyder, there are letters and numbers entered with a simple pencil: D.K. 30-9-99 24036

I don't remember how I obtained that book, and I don't know what these numbers really mean. The handwriting is unfamiliar. But they certainly mean something; something very significant, one more story, a symbol penciled into one of the greatest tales ever written in India. Both 'River of Fire' and the penciled note make one dream and to use imagination – to be alive.

As pornography could not be defined as love, the 'new stories' that shape our worldview and penetrate our psyche, are actually not true stories at all. They are substitutes that were implanted in order to replace permanently the real thing.

They kill life itself in the real living beings.

Those endless car chases, meaningless slaughters of thousands of humans in almost every film, never-ending computer generated disasters and horror scenarios, all have very little to do with real life.

The 'new stories' are more like some addictive substance, narcotics, cigarettes stuffed with chemicals, or very bad booze.

All over the world, billions of hooked viewers, adult and children, women and men, even elderly, are now watching the same rubbish, consisting of computer-generated plots and images, phantasmagoric scenarios.

As was the case with the CIA-run Paris Review, the storytellers have been encouraged to elevate form over substance. We are expected to 'become daring' by showing as many female genitals in our art, describing as many mind-blowing situations, inventing 'personal dramas' and epic quests for 'self-fulfillment'.

All calls for egalitarian society, for rebellion, revolution, for the end of neo-colonialism, of state terror, of propaganda, were turned to absolute taboo.

'Politics are boring' is one of the main massages we are encouraged to spread around.

Because people are not expected to mingle in 'what is not their business'. Ruling the world is reserved for the corporations and few gangsters with excellent PR. The voters are there only to give legitimacy to the entire charade. And if they don't, they get slaughtered like in that brilliant novel called "Seeing" by Portuguese novelist Jose Saramago.

Or as in real life, Europeans were massacred in France, Italy and Germany after the WWII, when they were going to vote Communists into power, but instead were confronted by old Nazis who were put to work by Western allies, concretely by the US and UK, to murder the leaders and supporters of the Left. Successful Nazis were then shipped, discreetly and with all that loot from Jewish victims, to distant South America, where I met and interviewed some of them and their children – in Paraguay, Chile, and Peru.

But don't you even think about writing stories about it.

"Colonia Dignidad!" I was then told by one of the editors of major German Magazine Der Stern, when I presented him with damning photos and true stories about the murderous German colony in Southern Chile. At one point he burst laughing: "Never again!"

Real stories have been ridiculing such arrangement of the world. True stories were always 'political', because everything that matters is actually 'political'. Education and medical care are political and so are housing, city planning, green areas, corruption, arts, religiousness or secularism, and therefore even love and how it can or cannot be expressed.

Great novels have always been political, and what we see now, their de-politicizing, is abnormal, even perverse, fabricated. Many great songs used to be political, and they still

10

are – in Latin America, in Russia, or in China.

Even Hollywood used to go political in some of its greatest films like "All President's Men", "Marathon Runner", "They Also Kill Horses", "The Way We Were", "Kiss of the Spider Woman", to name just a few.

The French cinema was political almost by definition and so was almost everything great coming from Latin American and Italian studious, directly or indirectly. And Soviets were telling their stories about saving the world from fascism, and about their attempt to build a classless society.

All that had to be stopped, by every means.

Lenin very correctly pointed out that film is the most important art form that can influence the masses. He knew it and spoke about it, but the Western regime made perfect use of that fact.

To make the world fragmented, to control it easily, the Empire made sure that intellectual exchange between the continents was decisively disrupted. Everything had to be rerouted through 'hubs', where the information and messages could be monitored, selected and finally modified. Such hubs were New York, London, Los Angeles, Miami; all depending on what parts of the world were to be influenced, and through what media.

Los Angeles is the center for visual indoctrinating and de-intellectualization, while Miami is, among other things, the center for extracting teeth and turning into brainless pop the most political music form on earth, salsa, which originally came from Cuba and the rest of Caribbean isles.

If not directly destroyed, most of the great mainstay stories from different parts of the world had to be thoroughly 'retold', and only then be re-distributed widely all over the world, in their shiny, new and useless form.

The punch lines of Russian, Japanese and French film masterpieces have been amputated by pathetic Hollywood remakes.

Anglo-Saxons were now the only ones allowed to present their version of the stories to the whole world. And they truly perfected that brainwashing, indoctrinating narrative for instant consumption by, by now, fully uniformed viewers all over the world.

The main goal is clear: to make sure that people would not think. They should not think when they read, when they listen to music, when they watch films. They should not think much at all: just to study their specialized fields, work for companies, consume, vote as they are told, and obey. Or else!

Now people worldwide have been fed by the same doctrines, as they were fed the same products. An entire new religion of 'coolness' and 'stigmas' was born, propagated by electronic and social media, in turn fueled by the major multi-nationals.

To be 'cool' was turned to very opposite of what it used to be for centuries. Now it meant not to think, to be like the others, to be 'light', to chat, to exchange meaningless messages and information, to desire the same products, to look the same, to accept what the Empire and market-fundamentalism were professing. Those few thinking beings were booed and expelled to the margins, since the very young age; they were humiliated and at the end forced to join the ranks.

The concept was simple: "we will make you stupid, uniformed, uninformed, unimaginative. Then, we will give you free choice, and it is likely that you will demand even more empty entertainment, more uniformity, more social media, more chemical dreams. You will not protest, you will not demand the change of system. You will work hard to make elites richer, and consume what you are told you should find desirable. Amen.

We – your regime and you – will then be locked in one perfect symbiosis".

It went further. At some point, the Western ideologues and their media outlets awarded themselves exclusive rights to judge, to erect moral concepts.

It is as if a gang of bandits invades some frontier town, kills hundreds of men, rapes women, and robs the bank. The next day, members of the gang catch some miserable bicycle thief who took advantage of the chaos. The thief gets tried and condemned to several years in prison for his 'terrible crime'. The bandits pose as heroes and saviors.

This, actually, would be an extremely good story to tell. The whole charade is so ridiculous, so transparent. But, shockingly, nobody is laughing, definitely almost nobody is laughing in the West!

* * *

One of the greatest films ever made – Kurosawa's "Seven Samurai" – got swiftly overshadowed by a Hollywood remake, the "Magnificent Seven", because it had to be the American cowboys, not Japanese samurais, who had the right to demonstrate a true moral standard to the world.

Of course, Kurosawa was a socialist realist, and his early scripts were totally unacceptable to the Western regime. It is also important to recall that Kurosawa, after the war, was busy searching for ways to avoid the censorship imposed on Japanese art and media by the US occupation administration.

Like films, also all those brilliant fairytales from all over the world had to be kidnapped, recycled, their teeth extracted, their social message reduced to zero. Disney had repackaged those mighty as well tiny creatures from all corners of the planet, into a horrid, fast food-concept of fairytales; it destroyed and humiliated them, turned them into pinkish and yellowish kitsch.

Even in those countries with ancient cultures and folklore, like Thailand and Indonesia, there is hardly anything left of the original legends: children are growing up fully dependent on mass-produced toys designed in computer workshops in the United States, instead of relying on their own storytellers and wonderful legends. It is the same as with the junk food, and later, cigarettes.

All identity is wiped out, all creativity and originality destroyed. Even original lullabies are now disappearing from many parts of the world.

* * *

Writers, thinkers, journalists, filmmakers – most of them, gradually – became obedient propagandists of the regime.

Thus the horrid prophecy of Orwell and Huxley materialized, quietly, without any major dramas or 'significant events'. Of course true drama – the slaughter of hundreds of millions of innocent men, women and children in all corners of the world – has been ongoing for centuries. But the victims were, as Orwell called them, un-people, so nobody cared.

Then suddenly, everything became constrained. The flow of stories virtually stopped. We don't know when exactly it happened. Nobody does.

* * *

I often think about true stories in these dark days of the Western talibanisation of the planet. I draw inspiration and optimism from them.

Not too long ago, just some twenty years back, in the early 1990s, I was just a kid, a young reporter, covering the South American continent.

I will never forget dynamism, zeal and courage of the people I encountered in Chile, Argentina, Peru and Colombia. My novel, my rebellious Point of No Return that is just now being re-introduced to English readers after being fully re-edited, was greatly influenced by those years spent in Latin America.

Chile and Argentina were just waking up from their terrible nightmares, from brutal dictatorships supported by the West. Both countries were trying to come to terms with their past, to rebuild their societies.

Peru was still consumed by a brutal 'dirty war'.

The stories were everywhere; they were searching for storytellers, competing for our attention, chasing us.

I was still based in New York then, where I knew dozens of aspiring writers and filmmakers, many of them continuously lamenting about 'not knowing what to write'.

These were the post-Reagan days, New York was atomized, fragmented, with miserable slums and homeless people everywhere; people rotting at the entrances to subways, men and women dying lonely deaths, abandoned by their families and society. But writers took the luxury of not knowing what to say!

This was the era when the Empire was consolidating its power abroad, from south and Central Africa to Southeast Asia and the Middle East. The Soviet Union, country where I was born, was decomposing after the Afghanistan trap, under the terrible reign of one naïve nitwit, and then under another one, a brutal notorious alcoholic and protégé of the West.

I was shuttling between awakening in Latin America and absolute stagnation in the West, where the writers were too busy suffering from identity crises to notice what was happening in the world!

* * *

I remember how ecstatic I felt high in the Andes. Of course, not because of the war, but thanks to the stories, an incredible amount of them, of which almost all were genuine.

There, the air was thin and so was Anglo-American propaganda. There, the stories were firmly in control of life.

People talked. I listened. It was how it always was, for millennia, and it all felt right. I learned how to tell the stories in the Peruvian and Bolivian Andes. I learned how to listen. Sometimes it took the entire night to hear one simple and short tale in a clay hut, but it was always worth it.

One night my English photographer and I left the city of Ayacucho in the middle of the night, both of us shaken to the core.

Just two days earlier we were stopped by the Shining Path, Sendero Luminoso, hastily tried at the side of the road, and then condemned to death. True, we managed to talk ourselves out of execution, explaining, honestly, our distaste for both the President Fujimori and Yankee imperialism. But we were still in shock, as our young lives could have just ended there, at the curb, in one instance.

Ayacucho means 'corner of death', it is a beautiful but cursed place high in the mountains, very indigenous and battered by centuries of colonialism and consequent feudal mores.

It was pitch dark, and we turned all beams of our Land Rover on, shaking from altitude sickness, driving fast in order to 'fly over' an uneven dirt road. We were on assignment for a big news magazine, and we were young, and definitely not quitters.

At one turn, an indigenous woman dashed under our wheels. She jumped, then knelt, begging. I slammed the brakes. This could have been a typical trap; and it could have been our end. But the woman was crying, in pain, she was heavily pregnant, indicating that she was entering labor. Then she joined her hands in one powerful plea.

We stopped. We had no clue what to do. Two hardened war reporters with a big car and all that equipment inside, totally helpless, clumsy, stupid when faced with new life that was demanding our assistance.

We literally carried her to the car, put her on the back seat and played, just to do something, some Chilean ballads from car stereo. We tried to make her feel better.

What followed was a mess, a total mess! And from that mess a child was born. A girl. She was born alive and she survived; we all made sure that she survived. And two of us, two not so tidy young men who were cracking terrible jokes just a few minutes before, while our eyes were glued to the dusty road at some 4.000 meters altitude, searching for deadly military patrols, were now jumping around that good-natured indigenous matron with red cheeks, cleaning sweat from her forehead, trying to be at least somehow useful.

Eventually we drove both of them – mother and her tiny

daughter – to the next village, where we found a willing midwife. As birth-assistants we absolutely failed, but for weeks we felt endlessly proud and the girl – the baby girl – still lives in my memory – as the most beautiful, the dearest child.

That was one of the greatest stories I ever encountered, simple and pure as a creek, back there, high in the mountains.

Later I saw similar scenes in the movies. The men helping were always sensible, comical, and absolutely unrealistic.

We were not really sensible at all. It was a war, a brutal war, and it was cold and a woman was probably abandoned by her man; kicked out from her house… It was not a happy story, but it was human and at the end, a good story, and it probably made both of us better men.

After that, I saw death on many, too many occasions, and it was necessary to see it. I don't regret seeing death, because that is how this world is arranged, and I can't write about things I have never witnessed.

Everyone who went to war knows that how it is shown in most of Hollywood films is simply a lie. I described the war in my Point of No Return, and I am describing it again, now, in detail, in my latest 1.000 page novel.

It is important to write about the war, about the stories that one experiences during the battle and in ravished cities and villages. Because almost all wars in the modern history are caused, are triggered by us, by the West. Because our 'culture', our brutality, our greed, caused hundreds of millions of lives to be lost, all over the world.

Our 'real' wars now became 'remote'. We invented carpet-bombing, we dropped an A-Bomb; we killed millions of men, women and children in Indochina. We killed them mostly with our flying monsters, dropping millions of tons of steel on poor hamlets and villages full of people who just wanted to be truly free – free from our dictates and from our terror.

And now we use drones. We don't even dare to fly that heavy metal shit, anymore.

All this, because we are cowards, and our culture is both that of despots and weaklings. And to realize it, the only way to understand it, is to read and to watch real stories of those whom we have been brutalizing and torturing.

But we don't want to. We close our ears with the palms of our hands. We refuse to hear them speak and laugh, we make sure not to hear them cry and scream. We are killing them, but we are doing it 'surgically', long-distance, while watching on television sets tarantulas consuming our cities, while stuffing ourselves on pre-fabricated food and buying toys for tiny children – toys that have no heart and no soul, anymore.

We have turned into total idiots, and we even kill like idiots.

Oliver Stone made films about how we 'fought' the wars. That was the closest to reality. It was also an exception, and many people did not like what they saw.

The Soviet people fought real war and they saved our planet. They also helped to liberate dozens of countries from Western colonialism. Without them, there would be no freedom in Africa, Middle East and most parts of Asia. But those facts are oppressed and can't be mentioned.

What also can't be mentioned is the heroic, and at the same time humble, involvement of Cuban people in the African liberation struggle.

Soviets also made great films about fighting and wining the war, and about saving us from fascism. "The Cranes Are Flying", "The Ballad of Soldier", "The Dawns Are Quiet Here", to name just some.

Those wonderful Russian stories are completely unknown, from films to modern novels, even those brilliant cartoons they made for children.

The West which, at the beginning, fought half-heartedly the German Nazis while simultaneously committing crimes against humanity in Africa, Middle East and Oceania, made sure that everything connected with heroic struggle of Soviet Russia was dragged through dirt, and later has been using the same tactics again China and Latin America, particularly Cuba.

Cuba is the greatest enemy, a country the West demonized and tried to destroy by chemical warfare, terrorism and relentless propaganda.

Why Cuba? Because Cuba has three things that Western regime does not have: it has heart, it has humanism, and it has guts.

* * *

Is there any true opposition, or even self-criticism in the West? Or is the West really increasingly resembling its ally from the old days – the Taliban?

No films depict the open racism of Winston Churchill and his theories regarding "the beastly lesser races", or many other colonial monsters like British PM David Lloyd George, who, while his country was bombing Iraqi civilians in the mid-1920s, killed an international proposal to ban aerial bombarding with the phrase "We have to reserve the right to bomb the niggers." Hardly any stories unveiling terror unleashed against the colonies, in practical terms against the entire world, are being allowed to domesticate in the psyche of Europeans and North Americans.

Busts and monuments to the worst racists and criminals are now decorating London and all major British cities, as are the statues of Belgian King Leopold II, a mass murderer responsible for the slaughter of 10 million Congolese people and for the chopping of hands of those who did not work fast enough to fill up his coffers, now scattered all over Brussels.

The greatest and the most frightening story, that of enslaving of the world by European and later North American tyrants, was never told. The stories of resistance against this unprecedented and ongoing terror are perpetually suppressed.

* * *

So here I am again, in Egypt.

One ugly armored vehicle is moving its cannon from left to right, as if searching for something, for someone. It passed me and I could clearly see the inside of its muzzle. It did not stop;

it ignored me, as I was not the one it was searching for.

I keep working, unhurriedly, photographing and filming, then photographing again. I work monotonously, each move calculated.

Then something hits my chest. I do not feel almost any pain, not much pain at all, just some.

I thought it was a bullet; they say one does not feel much pain in the first instances, during few seconds after being hit. I did not want to look down, because if I was hit by a bullet through the chest, it would be all over very soon: my insane life, all those adventures and battles I lived almost since I was a child. And so I kept working, by inertia.

There was disgusting smoke all over the street and soon I realized that I was not hit by a bullet, but by an empty teargas canister.

I was alive, and suddenly, as if to celebrate that fact, that miracle, my brain recalled the handwriting penciled into the last page of The River of Fire.

And I recalled the face of a girl, a maid called Ratan, from The Postmaster, the first of Three Daughters trilogy directed by one of the most brilliant filmmakers of all times – Satyajit Ray. I recalled her story, originally written by Tagore:

A new postmaster comes from Kolkata to a small village. Ratan, a maid, an orphan, is 'given to him'. He is kind to her; he does not beat her as the previous 'owner' did. But he is bored in the village. He begins to teach her how to read and write. He talks to her. They are scared of terrible storm, together. He falls ill. She moves to his house; she stays next to him, day and night, awake, and saves his life. She falls in love with him, although not one intimate word is uttered. He recovers. He decides to leave. A new postmaster arrives. She meets her love, on an empty road, as he is departing. She looks at him, for the last time. He stops, and then moves on. This, outside of India almost unknown frame, is one of the most beautiful moments in the world cinema.

'What a story', I think. 'What a tremendous story!'

The smoke was now covering entire surface of the avenue.

"What am I doing here?" I thought, just for a fraction of a second.

But subconsciously I knew: I was at the frontline, for years, fighting for survival of real stories. Those that are all around us: small but deep, frightened and humiliated by multi-million productions coming from Hollywood and Disney, with all their false pathos and noise, and lies.

As I watched the cannon, I thought that philosophers, not only storytellers, were 'out of vogue'. Both were assigned the identity of wooden toys, made with love but now obsolete, pushed to oblivion by hyper reality, by electronic media, which reduced emotions and human interaction to just a few abbreviated incoherent barks.

I pushed the shutter. My heavy professional still camera recorded a moment – a tiny girl clinging to her mom, teargas burning her eyes. But her story, her tiny and real story: how could it compete with some giant insects invading the earth; how could it compete with the horror of entire California falling of the cliff in those doomsday Hollywood movies.

What I was actually doing here was desperately trying to record last glimpses of humanity. The real pain, real longing, hope and yes, love.

In order to record all those disappearing stories, I kept moving in geographical extremes, in some of the most inaccessible parts of the world, in conflict and war zones. I was propelled by thorough spite for virtual reality, which was attempting to murder compassion, hopes, dreams, even love. And it went without saying that the virtual reality felt absolute spite for people like me.

I straightened my filthy shirt and checked my lenses. They were intact. Cameras were working. My body was working. The name of the girl in Ray's film was Ratan. The handwriting at the end of the River of Fire said: D.K. 30-9-99 24036. Whatever it meant.

The gun moved again, this time from right to the left. Again it did not stop. I was alive. And my heart was still on the left, where it belonged, and it was beating regularly, pushing red blood through my veins. And I was not going to stop telling 'real' stories, for as long as there was that naturally left-centered movement inside my swelling chest.

2

HOW THE WEST MANUFACTURES "OPPOSITION MOVEMENTS"

Government buildings are being trashed, ransacked. It is happening in Kiev and Bangkok, and in both cities, the governments appear to be toothless, too scared to intervene.

What is going on? Are popularly elected administrations all over the world becoming irrelevant; as the Western regime creates and then supports thuggish 'opposition movements' designed to destabilize any state that stands in the way of its desire to fully control the planet?

***

They are shouting and intimidating those who want to vote for the moderately progressive government that is presently leading Thailand. There is no dispute over the electoral process – voting is generally free, as both international observers and most of the local Election Commission members agree.

Freedom, legitimacy or transparency is not what is at stake now.

The rhetoric varies, but in essence, the 'protesters' are

demanding the dismemberment of the fragile Thai democracy. Most of them are paid by the upper-middle and upper classes. Some of them are thugs, many hired for around 500 Baht a day (roughly US\$ 15) in the villages of the restive southern provinces of the country. They are accustomed to the use of violence, their body language and facial expressions clearly show it.

Government officials of the legitimate government have to climb over blockades, or beg protesters to allow them to enter their own offices.

People who came to vote in the pre-election round were intimidated and insulted, and one man was almost strangled to death.

While life in the capital has been fully disrupted, the government does not dare to send in tanks or the police to clear the streets. It should. But it is too scared of the army and the monarchy – two pillars of this outrageous hybrid of savage capitalism and feudalism – comparable only to even worse regional nightmares, such as Indonesia and the Philippines.

It is all in the open now: the government speaks of its fear, while the military sends poisonous threats through the lackey media and through 'leaks'.

What is happening and what is at stake? The Prime Minister's older brother, Thaksin Shinawatra, while he was PM himself, attempted to bring in a modern capitalist system to this submissive and deeply scared nation. And not only that: he housed the poor, introduced an excellent free universal medical care system (much more advanced than anything ever proposed in the United States), free and very advanced primary and secondary education, and other concepts deemed dangerous to the world order, and to the local feudal elites, as well as the army.

Thai elites, whose love of being obeyed more than wealth, admired and feared, reacted almost immediately. The PM was exiled, barred from returning home to his country, and smeared. There were military coups, mysterious 'alliances', rumours, and 'secret messages' coming from a 'very high place'. There was outright killing, a real massacre, when the so called 'Red Shirts', supporters of Mr. Shinawatra (ranging from moderate reformists to Marxists) were butchered by snipers, some shot in their heads.

But the people, the poor, the majority of Thailand, particularly those from the North and Northeast, reacted in a stoical and most determined fashion. Whenever elections were called, whenever the regime outlawed the pro-Shinawatra political parties, the new ones emerged, and kept winning the elections.

In 2011, Mr. Shinawatra's sister, Yingluck, became Thailand's Prime Minister.

'Protestors' blocked several central arteries of Bangkok, declaring that "Thailand is not ready for democracy", and that "if elections should determine the country's future, pro-Shinawatra forces would keep winning".

That, of course, would be unacceptable to the elites and to many Western countries that have, for decades, benefited from the Thai feudal system.

One of Thailand's generals, 'refused to rule out the possibility of another military coup'.

What the opposition proposed was some hazy concept, of a government of technocrats, which would govern until Thailand 'is ready' to vote: read until people's power is broken and it would become certain that a pro-elites, pro-monarchy and pro-military government would be 'freely' elected.

In the meantime, thugs are blocking public streets; cultural centers but not malls. They are described as 'protesters' in both Europe and the United States.

And here we are coming to the core of things: The terror of the military and feudalism was dressed up in the clothes of rebellion, even revolution. It was given legitimacy, even a certain romantic flair.

Fascism is raising its ugly head, once again. And the West is fully aware of it, and in fact it is openly supportive of the regime that is now de facto governing Thailand from behind the curtains. Because it is the regime it helped to manufacture.

***

I left Bangkok and while in the air, one thought kept repeatedly coming to me: many of the places I had been writing about lately are living a very similar reality as Thailand is.

Those elected democratically, those progressive in their core, these governments all over the world have been under severe attacks by some armed thugs, bandits, and anti-social elements, even by outright terrorists.

I saw it on the Turkish-Syrian border. I heard the stories of many locals, in the Turkish city of Hatay, and in the countryside near the Turkish-Syrian border.

There, I was stopped, prevented from working, interrogated by the local police, army and religious thugs, when I was trying to photograph one of those 'refugee camps' built by NATO specially for Syrian fighters, who were housed, trained and armed in this area.

Hatay was overran by Saudi and Qatari jihadi cadres, pampered by the US, EU and Turkish logistics, support, weaponry and cash.

The terror these people have been spreading in this historically peaceful, multi-cultural and tolerant part of the world, could hardly be described in words.

Children from the borderline village described raids, theft and violence, even killing, by anti-Assad 'rebels'.

Here, and in Istanbul where I worked with Turkish progressive intellectuals, media and academia, I was explained to again and again, that the anti-Syrian 'opposition' has been trained, financed and 'encouraged' by the West, and by Turkey (a member of NATO), causing the death and destruction of millions of lives in the entire region.

As I write these words, RT is broadcasting an exclusive report from the Syrian city of Adra, the city that had been plundered and destroyed by pro-al Qaida and the pro-Western 'opposition' forces, including the Free Syrian Army.

This is the city where, allegedly, one month ago, people were murdered, stoned alive, burned in barrels, and beheaded.

Instead of stopping support for the racist, bigoted and extremely brutal Syrian 'opposition', Washington continues demonizing Assad's government, and threatening it once again with military action.

* * *

And those thugs, in the countries that elected their own patriotic or progressive governments, were hired by local elites on behalf of the Western Empire.

And before that, the so-called 'elites' were hired, funded, or at least trained/'educated' by the West.

On an 'intellectual' level, the private media outlets have been fiercely competing with each other, over which one would become more submissive towards the foreign handlers. The militaries and the most regressive feudalist, even fascist forces all over the world (see Ukraine, for instance) are clearly getting back into the saddle, benefitting and taking full advantage of the trend.

All this has been happening in different degrees and with variable levels of brutality, in Thailand, China, Egypt, Syria, Ukraine, Venezuela, Bolivia, Brazil, Zimbabwe and many other places all over the world.

Right after reading my article about the situation in Thailand, published on 30 January, my Brazilian reader reacted:

"Similar to our Brazil: though in a faded... somewhat lighter environment but substantially the same... the local elites, right now in January 2014, are doing whatever they can, to prevent the re election of Ms Dilma Roussef... You are an experienced Latin America´s observer, you know very well..."

The process, the tactics, are almost always the same: Western-paid media, or Western media directly, discredit designated popular governments, then 'scandals' are created, colors designated to some newly constructed 'opposition' movement, thugs selected and paid, and finally deadly weapons 'miraculously' appear at the 'protest sites'.

As long as the government is 'nationalist', really patriotic and defending the interests of its own people against international plunder, (not like the Abe's government in Japan which is peculiarly described as 'nationalist', but in reality it fully sides with US foreign policy in the region), it gets marked, and it appears on an invisible but powerful hit list, old-fashioned mafia-style.

I witnessed President Morsi of Egypt (I was critical of his rule at first, as I was critical of the government of Mr. Shinawatra, before real horror swept both Egypt and Thailand), being overthrown by the military, which, while in its zealous over-drive, managed in the process to murder several thousands of mainly poor Egyptian people.

I was then in Egypt, in and out, for several months, filming a documentary film for the South American television network, Telesur.

In disbelief and dismay I witnessed my revolutionary friends going into hiding, disappearing from the face of the earth. This happened as outrageously arrogant families cheered on the military murderers with no shame, openly.

The logic and tactics in Egypt were predictable: although still capitalist and to a certain extent submissive to IMF and the West, President Morsi and his Muslim Brotherhood, were a bit too unenthusiastic about collaborating with the West. They never really said 'no', but that had not appeared to be enough for the Euro-North American regime, which, these days, demands total, unconditional obedience as well as the kissing of hands and other bodily parts. The regime demands old-fashioned, Protestant-style obedience, complete with self-deprecation and a constant feeling of guilt; it is ordering true and 'sincere' servility.

It appears that almost no country, no well-liked government can escape annihilation, if it does not fully submit.

It went so far that unless the government in a developing countries such as Philippines, Indonesia, Uganda or Rwanda, sends a clear message to Washington, London or Paris that "we are here simply to make you, in the West, happy", it would risk total annihilation, even if it was elected democratically, even if (and actually 'especially if') it is supported by the majority of the people.

All this is nothing new, of course. But in the past, things were done a little bit more covertly. These days it is all out in the open. Maybe it is done on purpose, so nobody will dare to rebel, or even to dream.

And so, the revolution in Egypt has been derailed, destroyed, and cruelly choked to death. There is really nothing left of the so-called 'Arab Spring', just a clear warning: "never try again, or else".

Yes, I saw the 'elites' of Egypt dancing, and celebrating their victory. The elites love the army. The Army guarantees their continuous place at the zenith, their power. The elites even make their little children hold portraits of the military leaders responsible for the coup, responsible for thousands of lost lives, responsible for breaking the great hopes and dreams of the Arab world.

What I witnessed in Egypt was chilling, and it resembled the 1973 coup in Chile (a country which I consider my 'second or third home'); the coup, which I am not old enough to remember, but footage of which I have seen again and again, in silent and never diminishing horror.

'Or else' could be the torture and murder of people in Bahrain. 'Or else' could be Indonesia in 1965/66. Or it could be the 'collapse of the Soviet Union'. 'Or else' could be civilian airliners exploding mid-flight; a Cuban plane was destroyed by CIA agents. It could be ravaged Iraq, Libya, Afghanistan, or Vietnam, Cambodia and Laos, bombed into the stone ages. 'Or else' can easily be some fully devastated country like Nicaragua, Grenada, Panama or the Dominican Republic. Or 'or else' could mean ten million people butchered in the Democratic Republic of Congo, for both its natural resources and for the anti-imperialist outspokenness of its great leader, Patrice Lumumba.

Now in Egypt, Mubarak's clique is rapidly coming back to

power. He was a well-trusted 'devil', and the West quickly realized that to let him fall would be a serious strategic blunder; and so it was decided to bring him back; either personally, or at least his legacy, at the coast of thousands of (insignificant) Egyptian lives, and against the will of almost the entire nation.

The military of Egypt, of course, cannot be allowed to fall, either. The US has invested billions and billions of dollars in it, and the soldiers are now literally in control of half of the country. And it is a very reliable organization: it murders without scruple any being attempting to build a socially just society in this the most populous Arab nation on earth. And it plays with Israel. And it loves capitalism.

Two countries are separated by thousands of miles, and belong to two different cultures, located on two continents; Thailand and Egypt. In both countries, people spoke. They voted in their leaders. Not some Communist government, mind you: just a moderately socially-oriented one in Thailand, and a moderately nationalist/Islamic one in Egypt.

In both cases, the feudal and fascist elites went to work, immediately. Those that are behind them, that are financing them, and 'morally' supporting them, is, I believe, absolutely clear.

***

Ukraine is not a fresh victim of destabilization tactics of the European Union, which is so sickly greedy that it appears it, cannot contain itself anymore. It salivates, intensively, imagining the huge natural resources that Ukraine possesses. It is shaking with desire dreaming of a cheap and highly educated labor force.

European companies want to get into Ukraine, by all means. But one has to be careful not to allow the Ukrainian hordes to enter that sacred and thoroughly racist fortress – the European Union. Europe can plunder all over the world, but it is strict and brutal to those who want to get in and 'steal its jobs'.

Of course the EU cannot do in Ukraine, what it freely does in many places like the Democratic Republic of Congo (DRC). It cannot just come and pay some proxy countries, as it pays Rwanda and Uganda (that are already responsible for the loss of over ten million Congolese lives in less than 2 decades), to plunder Ukraine and kill almost all those people that are resisting.

Europe, again and again, for centuries, has proven that it is capable of massacring entire nations without the slightest mercy, (while showing almost zero historic memory) and with almost no moral principles, at least compared to the rest of the world. But it is canny, and unlike the United States, it knows plenty about tactics, strategy and PR.

What the EU did in Libya is clear. Anyone claiming that the United States is acting on its own, must be exercising enormous discipline not to see how closely linked are the interests and actions of the old and new usurpers of Africa, Asia, Latin America, Middle East, Asia and Oceania. France is acting, once again, as the arch neo-colonial thug, particularly in Africa.

But Ukraine is 'right there', too near geographically, to the EU itself. It has to be destabilized, but it all has to appear very legitimate. 'The rebellion', 'revolution', 'uprising of its people'; that is the way to handle things 'properly'.

More than a month ago, a bizarre deal was proposed, where European companies would be allowed to enter and clean Ukraine of its natural resources, but the people of Ukraine would not be allowed to even come and work in the EU.

The government, logically and sensibly, rejected the deal. And then, suddenly, Thai-style or Egyptian-style thugs appeared all over the streets of Kiev, armed with sticks and even weapons, and went onto trashing the capital and demanding the democratically elected government to resign.

The groups of thugs include many neo-Nazis, anti-Semites and common criminals. They are emboldened by the Thai-style fear of the Ukrainian government, to use force. They are setting on fire police officers, blocking and occupying government buildings, preventing the administration from serving the people.

Just as their 'orange' predecessors, they have been manufactured and carefully crafted, before being released into the wider world.

***

In Africa, just to mention a few cases, tiny Seychelles, a country with the highest HDI (Human Development Index by UNDP) has for years been bombarded with criticism and destabilization attempts. The Government provides excellent totally free (including medicine) medical care and free education. The people of Seychelles are well fed and housed. It is definitely not a perfect society, but, together with Mauritius, it is the best the African continent has to show. But that does not seem to be relevant.

Propaganda from outside, as well as the mainly British-sponsored opposition press, is trashing the system.

One wonders why, but then, on closer scrutiny and understanding of the Empire, things become clear: The Seychelles used to cooperate closely with both Cuba and North Korea, on educational fronts and in other fields. It was too 'socialist' for the Empire. And for those retirees seeking an exclusive hedonist lifestyle, it would be acceptable to be surrounded by blue and maybe even by brown, but definitely not by red.

Eritrea, dubbed as the 'African Cuba', may be a proud and determined nation, but it was designated as total pariah and outcast state by most of the Western powers. It was hit by sanctions and punished for who knows what.

"We are trying to be inclusive, democratic and fair", the Eritrean Director of Education recently told me, in Kenya. "But the more we do, the more we care about our people, the more infuriated Western countries appear to be."

He was a very wise man and so he did not appear to be surprised. Both of us were just 'comparing notes'.

Zimbabwe is another clear and extreme case. There, the West evidently and openly supports 'the opposition', against the government that is loved and supported by the great majority of citizens; the government of liberation struggle against colonialism and imperialism.

Provoked by outrageous lies disseminated by the mainly British mass media, I visited Zimbabwe last year, disputing point-by-point all the main propaganda points directed against Harare. Needless to say, my report, published by CounterPunch, created outrage against Western propaganda, all over the African continent.

The West builds and feeds 'rebellions' and 'opposition' against Venezuela, Bolivia, Cuba, Brazil, and Ecuador, to mention just a few countries high on its hit list.

In Venezuela, the US sponsored an aborted coup, and it directly pays for hundreds of organizations, 'NGO's' and media outlets, with the direct goal of overthrowing the revolutionary process and the government.

In Cuba, the people of this proud and humanist nation have been suffering for decades. They have been enduring what can only be described as terrorism against their beautiful country. The US and the West have sponsored invasions, terrorist acts, even attempts to influence weather patterns and cause devastating droughts. Crops have been poisoned.

Any Cuban 'dissident', any thug that takes up arms against the Cuban system and the government, would get immediate funding and support from the United States.

Even Western media outlets, performing secret polls in Cuba, often come to the conclusion that the majority of Cuban citizens support their system. But that only infuriates the West further. Cuban people are paying a heavy price for their freedom, for their pride, for their independence.

There are many other examples how the 'opposition' and terror against 'unpopular' (in the eyes of the West) governments are built.

Bolivians almost lost their 'white' and-right wing province of Santa Cruz, as the US supported, many say financed the 'independence movement' there, obviously punishing the extremely popular government of Evo Morales for being so socialist, so indigenous and so beloved. Brazil, in one great show of solidarity and internationalism, threatened to invade and rescue its neighbor, by preserving its integrity. Therefore, only the weight of this peaceful and highly respectable giant saved Bolivia from certain destruction.

But now even Brazil is under attack of the 'manufacturers of opposition'!

I don't want to write at length about China here, in this report. Readers are already familiar with my stand, but in summary: The more high-speed trains the Communist government builds, the more public parks, free exercise machines, more public transportation lines and wide sidewalks, the more it attempts to make medical care free for all once again, the more it attempts to make education free and public – the more it is being smeared and called 'more capitalist than capitalist states (while over 50% of country's production remains firmly in state hands).

Russia, like China, Cuba or Venezuela, is demonized relentlessly, every day and every hour. Any oligarch, any deranged pop figure, who criticizes the government of President Putin, is immediately elevated by the US, German and other Western governments, to the level of sainthood.

All this is definitely not because of the Russian human rights record, but because Russia, like the Latin American countries and China, is determinedly blocking Western attempts to destabilize and destroy independent and progressive countries all over the world. It is also due to the increasing influence of the Russian media, particularly RT (Russia Today), which became a commanding voice of resistance to Western propaganda. Needless to say, this writer is proudly associated with RT and its efforts.

***

It is certain that what the world is experiencing now, could be described as 'the new wave' of a Western imperial offensive. This offensive is taking place on all fronts, and it is rapidly accelerating. Under the proud Nobel Peace Price winner, Barack Obama and his closest European Neo-cons and 'socialists with brown insides', as well as the re-elected fascist Prime Minister of Japan, the world is becoming an extremely dangerous place. It feels like some frontier town invaded by violent gangs.

The biblical perception of 'those who are not with me are against me' is gaining new depth.

And be aware of the colors. Be aware of the 'uprisings', or anti-government 'protests'. Which one is genuine and which one is unnaturally created by imperialism and neo-colonialism?

It all appears to be extremely confusing to the majority of people who are getting stuffed on the corporate media feed. Actually, it is supposed to be confusing! The more confused people get, the less capable they are to rebel against real dangers and oppression.

But in the end, despite everything, on the 2nd of February, the people of Thailand voted! They climbed the barricades; they fought with those who were attempting to close polling stations.

And in Ukraine, the majority still supports their government.

And Venezuela and Cuba have not fallen.

And the jihadi cadres are not yet in control of Syria.

And Eritrea and Zimbabwe are still behind their leadership.

People are not cattle. In many parts of the world they are already realizing who their real enemies are.

When the US sponsored a coup against Chavez, the military refused to follow, and as a handpicked businessman was sworn-in as President, the military began moving tanks towards Caracas, in defense of the legitimate and elected leader. The revolution survived!

Chavez passed away, and some say that he was poisoned; that he was infected with cancer, that he was hit from the North. I don't know whether it is true, but before he died, he was photographed, bold and sweating, suffering from an incurable disease, but determined and proud. He was shouting: "Here nobody surrenders!" And this one image and one short sentence, inspired millions.

I remember, last year in Caracas, standing in front of a huge poster depicting his face, spelling out his words. I would thank him; embrace him if I could, if he were still alive. Not because he was perfect – he was not. But because his life and his words and actions inspired millions, pulled entire nations from depression, from gloom and doom, from slavery. I read from his face this: "They try to screw you by all means, but you fight... You fall but you fight again. They try to kill you but you fight... For justice, for your country, and for a better world." Chavez did not say this, of course, but that is how it felt, looking at his photograph.

By then, most of South America was free and united against Western imperialism, and hard to defeat. Yes, here, nobody surrendered!

The rest of the world is still very vulnerable and mostly in shackles.

The West is continuously manufacturing and then supporting oppressive forces, be they feudal or religious. The more oppressed people are, the less disposed they are to fight for justice and for their rights. The more scared they are, the easier it is to control them.

Feudalism, religious oppression and cruel right-wing dictatorships, all that serves perfectly well both the market fundamentalism of the Empire, and its obsession with controlling the planet.

But such an arrangement of the world is abnormal, and therefore temporary. Human beings are longing for justice and, in their essence, are a sharing and decent species. Albert Camus, correctly, arrived at the conclusion in his powerful novel "The Plague" (analogy to fight against fascism): "there is more to admire than to despise in humans".

What the West is now doing to the world; igniting conflicts, supporting banditry and terror, sacrificing millions of people for its own commercial interests, is nothing new under the sun. It is called 'ordinary fascism'. And fascism came and was defeated, in the past. And it will be again. It will be defeated because it is wrong, because it is against natural human evolution, and because people all over the world are realizing that the feudal structures that Western fascism is trying to administer all over the world, belong to the 18th century, not to this one, and should never again be tolerated.

Andre Vltchek

3

I AM SCARED,
THEREFORE I AM BRAVE!

Recently, my Italian translator, Giuseppe, wrote me an email. It was not a typical exchange, but quite an extraordinary personal query:

"Many see you as a very courageous person. They would like to imitate you at that, at least a little bit, but they feel they are not courageous, say, 'by nature' and they cannot learn courage. What do you think about that? Can people train themselves to be courageous?

I do not know how to answer this question in brief, and definitely not in the body of an email, not in just a few words. But the question is important, maybe essential, and so I decided to reply by writing this essay.

***

I have travelled the world, covering a myriad of conflicts, on all continents. I have written books, made films, and produced investigative reports

I have seen fear on the faces of men, women and children,

I have seen misery and sometimes I saw what could only be described as absolute desperation. I often sensed fear 'in the air', in so many corners of the globe!

Fear has been, naturally, omnipresent at all battlefields and in the areas of carnage and plunder, but also at 'not so obvious places', such as churches and family homes, and even on the streets.

I have been 'studying fear', trying to understand its causes, its roots. I always suspected that to define what triggers fear, what produces it, would be like coming at least halfway to containing it, destroying it, freeing people from its tyrannical claws.

There are, of course, many types of fear: from rational fear of direct violence, to some abstract, almost grotesque fear that is imposed on people by our political regimes and establishments, by almost all religions, and by oppressive family structures.

The second type of fear is purposefully manufactured and has been perfected throughout the centuries. How to use it effectively, how to maximize it, how to inflict the greatest damage, all of that is passed on from oppressor to oppressor, from generations to generations.

Fear is administered in order to stop progress, in order to choke dissent and to keep people in a thoroughly submissive and servile position. Fear breeds ignorance, too. It offers a false sense of security and of belonging. Needless to say that one can belong to an extremely bad 'club', or to a family of gangsters, or to a fascist country. Fear manipulates masses to an ignorant obedience, and then threatens those who resist: "don't you see, that is what the majority of people want and think. Follow the others, or else!"

***

Almost several decades ago, thinkers like Huxley, Orwell and others prophesied societies in which we now live. We are still reading '1984' or 'Brave New World' with disgust, and with outrage. We read those books as though they are some imaginary, science-fiction horror, not realizing that those nightmares, actually, have already arrived in our countries, cities, even into our own living rooms.

As many nations, including those in Europe and North America, increasingly succumb to indoctrination and intellectual homogeneity, courage is vanishing. It is demonstrated very infrequently, and it clearly fails to inspire the majority.

It is not because 'people have changed', but because the world in which we are living is becoming increasingly compliant and restrained, and the main sources of information (mass media), as well as those sources that shape public opinion and the behavioral patterns of the citizens (social media), are fully controlled by corporate and conservative political groups and their interests.

While people used to be influenced and inspired by great thinkers, novelists and filmmakers, they are now being shaped by 160-character messages of social media, and by all those opinion-formers who try to make them shallow, unemotional, compliant and cowardly.

In much of the distant past, but before I was born, rebellions and revolutions were seen as something truly heroic; they were respected and seen as something worth living for, even dying for. That was still the era of true pathos, of struggles against fascism and against colonialism. And life was not stripped of all poetry, yet, not even of revolutionary poetry.

One's worth was defined by one's contribution to building a much better world, not by the size of his or her SUV.

In those days, entire nations rose up from their knees. Great men and women led some of the spectacular rebellions. Writers, filmmakers, even musicians joined the struggle, or often marched at the vanguard. The line between top investigative journalist work and the arts became increasingly blurry, as great personalities such as Wilfred Burchett and Ryszard Kapuscinski circled the globe, relentlessly identifying its plights and grievances.

Life suddenly became meaningful. Many, not the majority but definitely many, were ready to dedicate their lives, and even to die, in order to destroy that outdated and unjust world order; to build, from scratch, a decent and prosperous society for all human beings, or in brief, 'to improve the world'.

If you see some of the French, Italian, Japanese and Latin American films from that era, chances are, that you will get goose bumps. Such was the energy, the zeal, and determination to challenge the establishment and to improve life on the planet.

When Sartre spoke, even if on topics such as imperialism and colonialism, hundreds of thousands of people would gather in Paris, and he would often appear in places like the Renault factory, far away from those famous intellectual salons of the capital.

"I rebel, therefore I exist!" wrote Albert Camus, proudly. It appeared to be one of the main mottos of that era.

Then, suddenly, rebellion ended', it was 'contained'.

But the wars continued. Imperialism and colonialism regrouped. Media outlets were purchased, bought. Capitalism won, once again, despite all dialectic logic against such a victory. Progress was stopped, even reversed. Corporatism produced Thatcherism and Reagan-ism, and the world got its shackles and muzzles back. Then, that gangrenous 'War on Terror' was launched and fear began creeping back, even from where it had been expelled several decades earlier.

***

I do not consider myself 'brave', Giuseppe.

In fact, I am very scared, and that is why I rebel, and risk my life, constantly.

I am scared of what I see. I am also scared of not being able to see, to witness, to document.

I am scared when I see the desperate faces of women, holding photos of their disappeared or killed husbands and sons.

I am scared of the aftermaths of aerial bombardment and of drone warfare.

I am scared of overcrowded hospitals, with injured people screaming on the floor, drenched in their own blood.

I am scared when I witness how all those great dreams of, on paper, independent countries in Africa, Asia, Middle East and Oceania are vanishing into thin air.

I am scared of all the new forms of imperialism, of neo-colonialism, of buying intellectuals in poor countries, of manufacturing 'opposition movements' against the governments the West does not like.

I am scared of the irreversible destruction of our beautiful planet. I have seen how entire stunning countries, atoll nations, are becoming uninhabitable because of global warming and the rising sea level – Tuvalu, Kiribati, and the Marshall Islands.

I am scared when I see scars instead of beautiful rainforests, stumps of trees and black chemicals floating where once ran bubbly, happy rivers – in Sumatra, Borneo, and Papua.

I am scared of so many things!

I am scared of seeing women being treated like dogs or doormats, as possessions of their fathers and husbands, and even brothers.

I am scared when brutal, corrupt and ignorant priests ruin lives and spread grotesque fears.

I am scared when books are getting burnt, directly or indirectly, replaced by sheets of metal and plastic, with potentially controllable content.

I am scared when they are, metaphorically or in real terms, shooting people straight between their eyes, or in their backs, simply because they refused to kneel.

I am scared when people have to lie in order to survive, or when they have to betray their loved ones.

I am scared of rape, of people being raped; in any way that rape is performed – physically or mentally.

I am scared of darkness. Not the one in the bedroom, at night, but of the darkness that is once again descending on our planet, and on humanity.

And the more scared I am, the more I feel that I have to act.

It is just because sitting still is the scariest thing of all. Sitting still while this world, this beautiful world which I know so intimately; from Tierra De Fuego to Northern Canada, from the Cape of Good Hope to the tiny Pacific Islands, to PNG to DRC, is being plundered, violated, and intellectually lobotomized.

It is also because I am a human being, one tiny grain of sand in this tremendous mankind, and as Maxim Gorky once wrote "Mankind – that has a proud sound!"

I am not always scared.

When the muzzle of a gun attached to some tank, slowly moves in my direction, I am not scared. I have seen what happens, what can happen if it fires; unfortunately I have seen it too many times. The moment of pain must be very intense but extremely short – and then, there is nothing. I don't want it to happen to me, because I love this life so passionately, so much, but I am not scared of the possibility of death.

But again, I am extremely scared of 'not being there', of not witnessing and documenting life, in its full beauty, in its richness and its brutality.

I am scared, I am terrified, of not knowing, of not understanding, of not fighting, of not rebelling, of not loving, not hating, not running, not falling, not laughing or crying (as one cannot exist without other), of not doing the right thing, or not erring, of not existing!

***

To search for the truth, to educate oneself, that is already brave, it is very brave.

The way our world is structured nowadays, people are strongly discouraged from being different.

Most men and women, even children, are now conditioned in such a way, that it makes taking the first step away from the controlled mainstream, extremely difficult. To step out of that 'comfort zone', away from the swamp of 'commonly accepted and promoted values', of cheap clichés, and the outright lies, is brave, heroic.

As a result, while the world is in flames, while it is being plundered, very few are actually fighting for its survival.

Has courage disappeared from this world? Is cowardice what actually accompanies those cheap 'pop' values'? Does shallowness, intellectual and emotional, breed compliance?

Can there still be a struggle for justice? Is rebellion still possible? Of course there can still be, of course it is, and you are walking away, you are rebelling as well, Giuseppe, with every article that you translate, and with every question that you ask.

It is not necessary to always face a combat helicopter, in order to be defined as a brave person. Some do go to wars, of course. I do. Is it because I am brave? Or is it because it is sometimes easier to point my camera at some battlefield, than to deal with the gentle art of translation? I don't know. Let others judge.

But to answer your question, it is: yes, one can learn the trade, any trade. And one can also learn how to be brave, too.

However, courage just for the sake of courage is worth nothing. It is like bungee jumping, or driving at breakneck speed on some icy road, not much more. Just a strong rush of adrenaline…

Genuine courage, I believe, has to have a purpose, an important goal. And to risk one's life, one has to really and deeply love it, and to respect it: his or her life, as well as the life of others. Therefore, courage makes sense only if it is there to protect the life of other human beings. One has to love this life, passionately and madly, in order to fight for it, in order to fight for the survival of others.

A courageous person can never be a slave, to anyone or to anything. Maybe that is the best way to begin 'being brave': by realizing, by defying, by demolishing slavery, by fighting against it no matter where and in which form it exists. There is still so much of it, all around us… Not only that old-fashioned slavery defined by shackles, but all types of slavery, in so many forms.

Accepting slavery, but especially becoming a voluntary slave, is the opposite of courage.

To 'swim with the flow', equals to being a slave. To repeat pre-fabricated clichés, to refuse forming his or her personal opinion is nothing less than intellectual servitude.

Of course, to be courageous, one has to be informed, as one has to be able to analyze the world, to choose a personal set of values, to be secure. Then and only then can one fight, if there is no other way; to fight and to risk everything combating oppression and brutality, whenever human beings are being tortured and violated, anywhere on this planet.

In order to be informed, one should never 'believe', one should always demand to know! That is brave too, and not at all easy, but necessary. It is brave when one is determinedly demanding to study and to learn, when one dares to form his or her own personal opinion. Not some pre-chewed school curriculum, but real learning. That is actually immensely brave, and also the only way to help to move humankind forward.

That is why truly free thought has lately been directly and brutally targeted in the West, and in the other oppressed parts of the world. Because this present regime, this 'New World Order', which is actually not new at all, is doing all it can to reverse natural development, to lock us all back in the gloom and doom of some outdated religious-style dogmatism. We are forced; we are being conditioned to believe in capitalism, in a Western style of 'multi-party democracy', in the superiority of Western concepts.

But it is clear – more thoughts are there, more alternatives, options, more checks and balances, the safer our planet becomes. Needless to say, it is brave to fight for its safety.

***

There is perhaps nothing as powerful, as humble, as honest, as this quote by Bertrand Russell displayed in the office of Noam Chomsky, at MIT:

"Three passions, simple but overwhelmingly strong, have governed my life: the longing for love, the search for knowledge, and unbearable pity for the suffering of mankind."

This quote also helps to answer the question posted by my translator and friend from Italy:

When the desire for knowledge becomes truly overwhelming, one simply cannot stop, or slow down. The only way is to go forward, to absorb knowledge, to fight for attaining knowledge, to see the world, to understand, to feel, to listen; passionately and consistently. No fear can deter us, when we are avidly searching for truth. It is so proud, so brave, this desire to know!

When we feel 'unbearable pity for the suffering of mankind', when we witness how unjust is the arrangement of this world, when we truly internalize the suffering of others, of our fellow human beings living on all the continents of this beautiful but battered planet, then almost all of us, or at least those who are humanists in their core, become courageous, and brave. They suddenly know what has to be done.

As for 'the longing for love', it is there, it is always there, in all of us, in all human beings. To fight for love, when it comes, is brave, and to die for it, if risking all is the only way to save it, is courageous. That 'longing for love' is the most humble, most sacred, the most essential part of our nature, so rarely satisfied. It takes courage to love; it takes tremendous, indescribable courage!

As the Cuban poet Antonio Guerrero Rodriguez, one of those brave 'Cuban Five', imprisoned for defending their country against Yankee infiltration and terrorism, once wrote: "Love is either eternal, or it is not love." If it can vanish, it is not love. El amor que expira no es amor.

These words, a poem, were written in a brutal North American prison and what they mean is clear. It is brave to love. It is so easy to betray. But it takes real courage to defend love.

Such courage, Giuseppe, can be learned. Or it can simply be discovered and nourished, as it lives inside us: inside all of us it lives!

4

JAPAN'S ODD PRO-WESTERN 'NATIONALISM'

Can one be a nationalist, while faithfully serving the interests of a foreign country or an empire? Anywhere else in the world the answer would be resolute and loud "No!"

It would appear as a clearly logical and linguistic contradiction. But in Japan, such a pirouette is apparently imaginable, acceptable and for many it is even perfectly 'normal'.

At Nashappu Cape, which is right outside Wakkanai, the northernmost city of Japan, huge radars and military listening devices have been humming for decades, their low-key electronics resounding day and night. They are pointed directly at Russia and its remote island of Sakhalin, a huge isle taken over by the then Soviet military at the end of WWII, possibly because of Moscow's fear that Japan would soon become a US colony. Having huge US military bases not far from the cities of Khabarovsk and Vladivostok did not, obviously, appeal to the Soviet Union, which had just lost approximately 20 million people, fighting and defeating fascism.

On any clear day, Sakhalin is visible from the shore, or from the windows of any Wakkanai's multi-story hotels.

Almost all signs in Wakkanai appear to be friendly towards visiting foreigners, as they are written in Japanese, English and Russian. But there can be no doubt: The city is firmly integrated in the massive imperial structure of the United States, based on the Asian continent. And Japan has been, since the end of the WWII, the most important element of this arrangement.

In Tokyo, I asked David McNeill, leading expert on Japan and Professor at Sophia University, whether Japan is really an independent country, when it comes to its foreign policy. He got straight to the point:

"Critics would say 'no', and I would be among those people... Japan, after the Second World War, aligned itself very quickly with America... And Japan's military alliance with America is also accompanied with, what critics would say, its subservient attitude towards Washington."

These days, Japan is in some sort of high or low level confrontational mode with almost all its neighbors. Cynics would say 'not surprisingly', considering that relations are strained between Japan's best friend the US, and China, Russia and North Korea.

Some 3,000 kilometers from Wakkanai, at the opposite end of Japan, the chain of Ryuku Islands is totally militarized by the US air force and marines. In fact, the bases occupy some 19 percent of the land of Okinawa, and fences and barbed wire fragment much of the rest.

"We are colonized; our land and even our minds are now colonized," explained leading Okinawan writer, Ms. Chinin Usii.

On a normal day, from two major US air force bases located on Okinawan soil – Futenma and Kadena – jet fighters and surveillance airplanes take off with deafening regularity, innerving both China and North Korea. Okinawa itself suffers: the F-15's fly at extremely low altitudes, their engines roaring.

The island feels humiliated, used, sacrificed by Tokyo.

The governor of Okinawa was supposed to have kicked the military bases off the island, but at the last moment, he succumbed to pressure from Tokyo and, according to most local residents, 'betrayed Okinawa.'

The more it loses out economically to China and South Korea, and the more irrelevant it becomes politically, Japan becomesincreasingly frustrated and aggressively pro-Western, particularly pro-United States. And what better way to show loyalty than by keeping those enormous US air force bases on its soil, especially if the soil is one thousand miles from Tokyo, and belongs to islands with a distinct identity and culture.

'Becoming more and more pro-Western'

"There is this very strange mood in Japan these days," explains Osaka-based film editor, Hata Takeshi. "Japan is becoming more and more pro-Western, while increasingly showing anti-Korean and anti-Chinese sentiments."

This is reflected in several opinion polls, showing that most Japanese people now view the West favorably, and its North Asian neighbors negatively.

The incumbent administration is not only hawkish, it is brazenly insulting towards China and Korea. For example, Prime Minister Abe was unrepentant when he visited the ill-famed Yasukuni shrine recently, a place where many Japanese war criminals are buried.

Japan is increasing its military budget, and there is a strong drive to revisit, reverse, or at least to amend its peaceful post-war Constitution. Abe is talking tough; he is promising 'change'. But the 'change' could trigger conflict in East Asia.

Japanese Self Defense forces aircraft regularly fly over the disputed islands, outraging China. These dangerous games are backed by the US, which is backing Japan with strategic bombers.

In the meantime, the coverage of these events by most of the mainstream Japanese media is thoroughly one-sided and anti-Chinese as well as pro-Western, in its tone and core. China is accused of 'belligerence' and 'aggressiveness' when it comes to recent events surrounding the disputed Senkaku Islands [known as Diaoyu in China] and such definitions are almost never challenged in public.

The fact that Japan is upsetting fragile a status quo and, according to many analysts based in Asia, is actually 'provoking China', is very rarely mentioned on Japanese TV or in the pages of its most widely read newspapers.

Reports by the Japanese media increasingly resemble a well-orchestrated propaganda drive. On February 13th, The Japan Times offered a predictable and stereotypical summary of the events, related to China and possible changes to Japan's Constitution:

"Prime Minister Shinzo Abe, pressed by China and seeking to strengthen ties with the US, is considering Japan's biggest change in military engagement rules since World War II. Having increased the defense budget two years running and set up a US-style National Security Council, Abe is now seeking to allow Japan to come to the aid of its allies. China's escalating challenge over the sovereignty of the Senkaku Islands has played into Abe's plans to strengthen the Self-Defense Forces," says Liberal Democratic Party lawmaker Katsuei Hirasawa.

Militarizing Japan

Leading Australian historian and professor emeritus at Nagasaki University, Geoffrey Gunn wrote about the questions and answers sessions at the Japanese House of Representatives Budget Committee on February 12, 2014, an event that had scant coverage in local and international press. Gunn watched the session with his wife on local TV.

"Prime Minister Shinjo Abe sat in the front row, occasionally taking the microphone. Deputy Prime Minister, Taro Aso, reclined beside him. At the podium, following a round of applause, came Shintaro Ishihara, the unreconstructed neonationalist former governor of Tokyo. In his present incarnation, Ishihara enters the picture as member of recently resigned Osaka mayor and right-wing ideologue Toru Hashimoto's Japan Restoration Party (Nippon Ishin no

Kai). Also taking the podium was defense minister, Itsunori Onodera, fresh from a visit to India drumming up security and defense ties with China as the obvious target," Gunn said about the session. He noted that Ishihara is the one who, by threatening to "purchase" the Daoyu/Senkaku Islands, forced the hand of the then government to nationalize them, thereby breaking with the status quo of recognizing a dispute with China as the other claimant, and setting up a dangerous escalation in tensions between the two nations.

"Far from backing off, the octogenarian Ishihara launched into a 30 minute harangue, denying the legitimacy of the Tokyo War Crimes Trials; calling for an expanded 'Self Defense Force' (the full nuance of his demands escaped my interpreter); making a pitch for the purchase of attack fighter aircraft; and virtually beating the drums of war," Gunn noted.

"For Prime Minister Abe, whose recent visit to the Yasakuni Shrine (inter alia, a shrine honoring A-class war criminals) offended both China and South Korea, Ishihara offered the soothing words, 'don't hesitate to visit again and ignore the words of neighboring countries.'"

"Defense Minister Onodera, Prime Minister Abe, and Ishihara appeared to be in concord, a veritable cauldron of hawks. Gaffe-prone Taro Aso slumbered on, fortunately, perhaps, as the world cannot forget his statements of the previous year that a Nazi-style Reichstag would be the appropriate way to ram through constitutional amendments to better fit the Abe government's neonationalist agenda. All I can say is that if the military attachés of concerned states, Washington included, were not watching this show then they should have been," Geoffrey Gunn wrote.

The atmosphere in Japan at this time, as the Asahi newspaper reported, is that books and periodicals highly critical of China and South Korea are flying off bookstore shelves, prompting leading publishing companies to jump on the bandwagon to take advantage of the trend. But despite the undeniable turn towards the right, the Japanese public still disapproves of Abe's plan to change the pacifist course, and the Constitution. According to a poll conducted by Kyodo News, at the end of January 2014, approximately 54 percent of Japanese citizens expressed their dissatisfaction with the potential changes.

But while the majority of Japanese people would not like to see their country turning back and once again becoming a major military power, hardly anyone thinks of criticizing Japan's alliance with the United States.

In Okinawa, a former US marine who became a leading academic, Douglas Lummis, recently explained:

"The other day I heard, in open forum, two ladies discussing whether Japan's peaceful Constitution should be nominated and granted intangible world heritage status. They asked my opinion... I said: 'But while Japan has a peaceful Constitution, it allows huge US military bases on its territory. And these bases are anything but peaceful. And there is this military alliance between the two countries...' They could not understand my point: to them and to many Japanese people, challenging the US-Japan military alliance would be something thoroughly unthinkable. I totally confused them."

It is perhaps not Japan itself, but its alliance with the West that is threatening peace in Northeast Asia.

The peaceful Constitution may still become, one day, an intangible world heritage. And Japan's self-defense force may not shoot at anybody abroad for some time to come. But what purpose would all this serve, if US strategic bombers take off one day and head towards China, North Korea, and even Russia, from those enormous military airports based on Japanese soil?

5

SOON, THE BATTLE FOR VENEZUELA

They are already sewing your funeral gown, Venezuela. They are now ready to welcome you back to that world of the lobotomized, destroyed nations that are fully submissive to Western political and economic interests – Indonesia, Philippines, Paraguay, Uganda, Kenya, Qatar, Bahrain, and almost the entire Eastern Europe. There are so many places like that – it is impossible to list them all.

They want you back in their deadly embrace; they want you to be corrupt and hopeless, as you were before the "Bolivarian Revolution".

They want you to be the top oil exporter, but with all those horrific slums hanging, like relentless nightmares, over your cities. They want your elites and your military top brass to speak English, to play golf, to drive luxury cars and to commit treason after treason, as they used to commit treason for decades, before your brave predecessor, President Hugo Chavez, began serving and literally saving the poor, in Venezuela and all over Latin America.

Those who are planning to destroy you, those who belong to the so called 'opposition', in their heads, are already portioning you; they are dividing your beautiful body – fighting over which parts should be taken where and by whom. They are arguing which pieces of you should stay at home, and what should be taken abroad – a leg, an arm, and your deep melancholic eyes, the color of the profound pools under the mighty waterfalls of Canaima. They want to sell your jet-black hair, as black as those evenings in the mountains, or like that endless night sky above Ciudad Bolivar.

They want everything, all that is under your skin as well as what is deep inside your body. They want your skin, too, as well as your heart.

They want your dreams, which are almost everybody's dreams – the dreams of all those people from all over the world, people that have been oppressed, and humiliated, for centuries, up to today. They want to take your dreams and to step on them, dirty them, spit on them and to crush them.

But it is not over; it is all far from being over. You are loved and admired, and therefore you will be defended. By all means – we who love you will not be ungenerous; we will not be negotiating the price!

For many men and women, for millions all over the world, you used to be a girl; a brave, rebellious, wonderful young woman... then suddenly you became a mother and then you turned to a motherland – for all those who lacked one until this very moment. For me, too, you became a motherland... for me too!

***

I am not a Venezuelan citizen. I wish I could be, but I am not. But I have fought for Venezuela, in my own way, through my reports and speeches, through films and in my books. I fought ever since Hugo Chavez became the President, 'my President'.

And I am proud that I fought. And now, when Venezuela is

once again under vicious attack, I want to stand firmly by her side, by the side of her Revolution, by the side of El Processo, and of her great Presidents – both Chavez and Maduro!

And I want to say this, and I will say this loudly, carajo: I don't care what passport is hanging from my pocket, but Caracas is now my capital, and Caracas is what we are going to defend, if we have to. Because in Caracas, we will be fighting for Havana, for Harare and Johannesburg, for Cairo and Calcutta, for the tiny atoll nations in the Pacific Ocean, for Hanoi, for Beijing, and even for Moscow, Asmara, La Paz, Valparaiso, Quito, Managua and for so many of the other independent, freedom-loving places of this wonderful world.

The violent activities undertaken by those so-called 'protesters' in Caracas have to be stopped, immediately, and if necessary, by force.

'The opposition' has been paid from abroad, as it has been paid, in the past and now, in China, in Eastern Europe, in Syria, Ukraine and in Thailand, as it has been paid everywhere else in the world, where the West could not manage to easily strip those 'rebellious' countries of all their riches, while keeping them humiliated, and on their knees.

***

As you are contemplating your next step, Mr. President Nicolas Maduro, as Venezuela is once again bleeding, as none of us knows what the next day may bring, I am leaving Indonesia, flying to Thailand. (For now it is Thailand, but I soon may change my course).

Thailand is not Venezuela, but their government also introduced free medical care and free education, and other basic social services. People responded – by supporting progress. They have been supporting it for years, through ballots.

But the elites intervened and the army intervened. There was a coup, and there are now voices shouting that 'the people cannot be trusted', otherwise they will always be voting for this administration, read: for progress.

The West is firmly behind the elites and against progress. Thai feudal leaders are fully trusted in Washington, in London, and even in Tokyo. It is because they have totally sold out their souls, because they fully lost all their shame during the Vietnam War. They fully participated in the horrible slaughter of the Vietnamese, Laotian and Cambodian people, and they even eagerly murdered their own people: revolutionaries, Communists and students.

The West likes it when such despots hold the reins of power. They like people like Duvalier, Trujillo, Videla and Pinochet – and their equivalents – on all the continents and in every country.

In Thailand they are now supporting the 'opposition', as they supported the 'opposition' in Chile before 1973 or in China before Tiananmen Square. As they are right now supporting 'the opposition' in Venezuela! Everything that can damage or destroy a rebellious country, Communist or non-aligned, goes!

It does not matter how many millions will die in the process. As long as a rebellion, or a fight for independence, can be crushed, Western imperialism and neo-colonialism will sacrifice any amount of human lives, especially the lives of those 'un people', just to borrow from the Orwellian lexicon.

I am soon leaving Indonesia, Comrade President Maduro. Indonesia is the country about which I have written books and made films, including a recent film for TeleSur.

Here, too, the West disliked the progressive President, Sukarno, who used to scream in face of the US Ambassador: "To hell with your aid!" Sukarno was one of the founders of the Non-Aligned Movement. Some would call him the Asian Chavez, and they would not be too far off the mark.

And so in 1965, the West teamed up with the local military and religious cadres, supplying them with lists of those 'who had to be killed'. What followed was one of the bloodiest coups in human history: between one and three million Communists, intellectuals, trade unionists, teachers and people belonging to the Chinese minority, were slaughtered. Culture was destroyed. The spine of the country was broken. It is broken right until now. It is terrible, a terrifying sight!

Now Indonesia is a servile, nauseating place, corrupt, both financially and morally. Its people are only there to supply multi-national companies and the local 'elites' with raw materials, and a low quality uneducated cheap work force.

It is exactly what the West wants to turn Venezuela into – the Latin American Indonesia, or even more frighteningly, the Latin American version of the African horror story – the Democratic Republic of Congo.

Venezuela's riches under and above the ground, are so numerous, and its land so fertile, its rainforests endless. Foreign companies and governments from the North simply cannot stop shaking from the lowest type of desire; unable to contain their unbridled greed.

The West, of course, does not come and say: We will rob you and rape you. They sing some stereotypical tunes about freedom and democracy. But anyone in Venezuela who wants to know what will happen to their country if the 'opposition' takes over, should go to Indonesia and see with his or her own eyes. Or should at least remember what occurred in the Chile of 1973, because in Chile, the US replicated its horrible Indonesian formula.

It is all connected and inter-connected, comrades, although Western mass media does not want us to know any of this.

***

Venezuela has to fight back! It is under siege and you were democratically elected, Mr. President. You have a mandate, and an obligation to defend your people.

I have worked in almost one hundred and fifty countries. And I have seen the horrors of those places that fell into the hands of Western usurpers: directly or indirectly. I have worked in places as diverse but broken as Paraguay, Honduras, Egypt, Bahrain, Kenya, Uganda, Philippines, Indonesia, the

Democratic Republic of Congo and the Marshall Islands.

Countries are so often punished for their great leaders!

In Congo, Patrice Lumumba decided to dedicate his life to feeding the children of the continent, to use the enormous natural wealth of his country for the good of his citizens. He despised colonialism and he openly repeated his accusations again the former colonial masters (the Belgians murdered ten million Congolese people during the reign of the Kind Leopold II) and against the neo-colonial clique. And he was murdered; after the Belgians, North Americans, Brits and others joined forces and decided that 'such behavior' could not be tolerated.

Now the DRC, country which has some of the greatest natural wealth on this planet, has the lowest 'Human Development Index'. Brutal Western allies in Africa – Rwanda and Uganda – have plundered DRC since 1995, on behalf of Western companies and governments. By now around eight million people have died. I made a film about it. Needless to say, nobody in Europe or in the United States wants to see it!

It is all because of Coltan, Diamonds, Uranium and Gold. But it is also, undeniably, because Congo once so proudly stood up against imperialism and foreign oppression. The Empire almost never forgives!

The Empire never forgave Yugoslavia, another founding member of the Non-Aligned Movement, breaking it apart and bathing it in blood. It never forgave Russia, supporting an awful despot and alcoholic, Boris Yeltsin in his determined efforts to ruin what was left of the Union of Soviet Socialist Republics, and by murdering thousands of Russian people during the siege of Russian 'White House'.

It never forgave China, or North Korea, or Zimbabwe.

The list goes on, and it is endless.

Please, do not allow this to happen to Venezuela!

Allende, Sukarno and others, fell, and their countries fell, because they assumed that despite everything, despite the West murdering hundreds of millions of people all over the world, for many centuries, it would actually not be as brutal in this particular day and age, it would at least spare cities such as

Santiago or Jakarta.

Then, when millions of Indonesian women had been gang-raped, when their breasts were 'amputated', when victims had to dig their own graves before being killed... when Chilean women were violated by dogs, under the supervision of 'English speaking investigators' as well as old German Nazis from Colonia Dignidad, when people were "disappeared", tortured, thrown alive from the helicopters... Mr. President, it was too late... Too late to fight!

***

I saw enough of this. As a war correspondent, as a man who was searching for the truth on all continents, writing about the most devastated cities and nations, I managed to absorb so much pain and suffering that I hope it gives me at least some right to write this letter, this appeal, and to urge you: "Do not allow this to happen to Venezuela."

Those who are opposing you will not stop – they will go all the way, if allowed. They have been engaged in a disinformation campaign, suspiciously similar to the one before the "9/11" in Chile, 1973. The 'strikes' and 'insecurity' are also similar to those provoked in Chile and Indonesia before their coups. And like elsewhere, in Venezuela there is also a group of 'economists' and 'business people', ready to reverse the course of the country, immediately, were the counter-revolution to succeed.

It is great business to oppose you! Tens of millions of dollars are poured into the coffers of those who want to overthrow the government of Venezuela... of Cuba... of China... of Iran, Bolivia, Ecuador, and so many other countries...

But Venezuela is now so high, perhaps at the top, of the Western mafia-style hit list.

In my recent essay: "How the West Manufactures 'Opposition Movements'", I gave a list of countries where all this is happening right now – an attempt to use local gangs to

61

overthrow totally legitimate governments only because they are defending the interests of their people.

Mr. President, your country – Venezuela – is much more than a beautiful place inhabited by brave people. It is also a symbol of hope, and as Eduardo Galeano once told me in Montevideo: "To take away hope is worse than murdering a person."

Do not allow them to choke this hope: the hope of the Venezuelan people, and the hope of millions all over the world.

If you have to fight, please fight! And we will join you; many of us will. Because what your predecessor and friend, Hugo Chavez, started, is what billions all over the world desire and dream of.

Venezuela, your Venezuela and my Venezuela, gave free books to the poor, free medical care, education, and housing to all needy people. Not as some sort of charity, but as something they deserve, have right to. Venezuela built cable cars, libraries and childcare care posts to help working mothers, where only naked misery reigned before. Venezuela educated and inspired some of the greatest musicians on earth. It stood against imperialism; it redefined, together with Cuba, what is 'heart' and what is 'courage'.

Now our Venezuela cannot fail. It cannot fall. It is too big, too important. Perhaps, the survival of the human race depends on the survival of Venezuela and the countries related to it.

After Hugo Chavez died, or as many believe was killed in cold blood, I visited TeleSur in Caracas. In the center of the city, there was a photo of Chavez, sweating, clearly suffering from chemotherapy, but clenching his fist: "Here, nobody surrenders!"

And a short distance away, there was another poster only showing a sprinkle of blood on a white background. 'Chavez from his heart', it read. Chavez was endorsing Maduro, posthumously.

President Maduro, let's defend our Venezuela! Please let us

not allow this revolution to fail. Let us do it by reason and by force! Let us do it for every tiny village destroyed by drones, for children dying from depleted uranium, for the 'Cuban 5', for those who died from the horrors of modern-day imperialism, in Congo, Angola, Vietnam, Laos, Indonesia, Iraq, Libya, Chile, and in dozens of other ruined countries.

Let us defend Venezuela for the sake of the humanity. No pasaran! This time, let us make sure that the fascist forces will not be allowed to advance!

Andre Vltchek

6

SHAMEFUL, COWARDLY EUROPEAN ART

I searched for pain, and I found none.

In those enormous halls of the Louvre, I searched for reminders of the agony of the people from the Caribbean, from islands like Grenada, where the native people were entirely exterminated during the French colonial onslaught. I searched for at least one tear, one moan, one canvas saturated with sadness and remorse. I searched for confessions.

But I found none.

I was trying to catch a glimpse of the desperate, terrified facial expressions of North African women, dragged into some empty rooms, and raped brutally by French soldiers. I was looking for paintings depicting the torture of Vietnamese patriots, and their execution by decapitation, for nothing else other than fighting for freedom and for their fatherland, against the appalling French colonial rule.

No – I found nothing, nothing at all in the Louvre, or in any other major French museums.

I stood in front of bizarre, sick and cold religious artwork, full of adult looking, perverse baby Jesus's, or of some saints with daggers sticking out grotesquely from their heads. It was mostly total kitsch, created to order from the Christian church – a morally corrupt religious entity responsible for the extermination of entire nations, of entire races, worldwide!

I could find no paintings depicting the destroyed people of Rapa Nui, no killing of Southeast Asians, Africans and the islanders from both the Atlantic and Pacific oceans.

I have searched and searched, for years, during my ever decreasing in frequency visits to that old and sick continent, responsible for dozens of holocausts on basically all the continents of the Earth.

Then, one day, recently, when I was presenting my documentary film (on Western-backed tyranny in Indonesia) at SOAS in London, I asked my mother, a renowned painter and cartoonist, to join me, and to search some more, just in case I have been missing, or overlooking, something substantial.

***

We spent days, crisscrossing several major museums in Paris, but we found nothing there, nothing in the Louvre.

Earlier we had found nothing in the State Gallery of Stuttgart.

And I found nothing in the Royal Academy of Art in London, or in the National Maritime Museum, or in the National Art Museum in London.

Not one excuse, not one apology, not a glimpse of remorse. I found no soul-searching, not even an enormous, erect, shouting question mark.

Brainwashed, corrupt and arrogant, European art has stood proud and unapologetic, unmoved by the suffering of those hundreds of millions of people who lost their lives because of those who patronized and funded most of the artists for centuries – the Christian Church, and the European political and economic establishment.

There has been no artwork depicting the torture and humiliation of entire nations; the vanishing of numerous great civilizations in Latin America... as there appeared to be no canvases illustrating entire Ukrainian villages burnt to ashes during WWII, or of the savage bombing of Leningrad, or of the medical experiments performed by German Nazis on human beings. Enormous canvases showing the holocaust against the Herero people of what is now Namibia were nowhere to be found.

I am not exaggerating, I honestly searched, but I found nothing remotely accusative, outraged, or furious at the Western torment of the world that has been going on for centuries, even millennia...

I found nothing brave or courageous, and nothing revolutionary whatsoever in the galleries of Stuttgart, or in the museums, exhibition halls, galleries of Paris and London.

I found no *j'accuse*. There was no scream and no agony, no suggestion that the West should be held responsible for all those crimes it has been committing. In all those European 'temples of culture' – all guilt was banished, as all the terror imposed on the world from Washington, London or Paris, was completely ignored.

I faced no images of the impact of the carpet-bombing on the Vietnamese villages, and no images depicting the rape of Algiers. I did not even see the suffering of Palestinian people – no artwork depicting it – or that total and quite well documented, recent destruction of countries like Libya, or Syria or the Democratic Republic of Congo.

On the paintings at the Tate Modern or at those countless Parisian galleries that I have been visiting, there were no images of women with their breasts cut off- a common occurrence during the Western-backed 1965 military/religious coup in Indonesia, which took at least one, but perhaps three million human lives – or of the women savagely gang-raped and mutilated in the DR Congo, where between six to ten million people have lost and are still losing their lives, in order to satisfy the unbridled greed of numerous Western companies, governments and consumers – greed for Coltan, Uranium, Diamonds and Gold.

Western art generously forgave everything; all the crimes committed by the Western Empire. Yes, everything is forgotten and forgiven... as it always is by the establishment itself; by the Western regime imposed so completely on our planet.

Bunches of forgiving blokes are now running museums and galleries. Stunningly 'forgiving', are the great majority of Western artists themselves, who are paid/rewarded generously and glorified relentlessly for such 'bigheartedness'. Just as they always have been remunerated for centuries, because, they agreed to put form over the substance.

Just keep painting countless cans of mass-produced soup, while your country is murdering millions of innocent men, women and children, and you will be elevated to a deity, by the regime.

Because the regime and the art establishment are one single entity! And they don't want you to be political, politicized, well informed, or angry with what your government is doing to the defenseless people of the world. And they don't want you to, god forbid; suggest that the masses should be informed and outraged!

Just entertain, spread your colors on huge canvases, and enjoy all those great privileges!

***

During my life, I saw many; too many destroyed lives, I saw craters and burning cities, and I saw women – too many women – victims of savage rapes. I saw pain and despair scarring countless monstrous, overpopulated cities, as well as vast and impoverished countrysides. I saw misery and indescribable sorrow on all continents, and on too many occasions.

But during these last ten days in Europe, I saw many endless lines, numerous ovals, and squares. I saw orange triangles and pink dots, as well as fluorescent disconnected words and grotesque bizarre objects... and I saw meditations on space and on failed erections... on multiple orgasms and on rubbish, shit and gore.

I observed ego trips and psychedelic LSD visions. I witnessed sex in many different forms. I saw countless studies on parents and their children: conflict between different generations... I saw emptiness.

I found it difficult to recognize the world, in which I was living – to recognize it in the Louvre, in British museums, and in several German museums... As I previously found it difficult to recognize it in Spanish museums, in Belgian museums... and in hundreds of contemporary art galleries all over Europe...

Nothing appeared to be recognizable.

I was not asking, I would not dare to ask, for outright realism, or naturalism... I was not demanding Socialist Realism. For now I was only longing for at least some links between the 'flights of insane fantasy' and the universe inhabited by human beings... I was yearning for some sense and some logic, for something that could serve our humanity, something that could enrich and improve the lives of millions of people.

But all that was flying into my face, were vulgar and egocentric concepts; art for art's sake... or some primitive and frivolous entertainment genres – the best allies of the Empire which was now willing to pay any amount of money just to convert human beings into some empty, emotionless and unthinking organisms.

***

For several long centuries, most West European art has been corrupt, prostituted and rendered toothless.

Lately, it has become out-rightly poisonous, anti-humanist and anti-human, deadly.

During those ten days that I spent in Europe searching for 'courageous art', I kept hunting for life, for real life, and for genuine feelings...

In between self-serving cacophonies of colour, I struggled to recognize some elements of great the Mexican murals and Soviet political posters... But there were no Diego Riveras and no Siqueiros.

Instead, there were countless phantasmagoric ego trips... There were lunacies and they were all supposed to entertain me, to impress me, to keep me floating in some abstract, cold but metallically cool, and always detached realm. But there was no strife for building a better world, no optimism, and enthusiasm, like in the great post-war paintings created in Vietnam, the Soviet Union and China.

Cynicism, detachment and selfishness – these all were promoted, paid for, and in vogue.

I desperately wanted to smell, I wanted to feel, to love fully and passionately, to hate, to struggle... I wanted all this, as almost every human being does want all this... as almost every man, woman and child wants to... even if secretly... even if shyly and subconsciously... in every society.

"We shall be returning to the simplest of the roses", a great Czech poet Jaroslav Seifert wrote in his unforgettable poem.

But almost all simple roses seemed to be gone; they have disappeared, faded away.

Everything was diverting me, taking me far away from reality... The art was grotesquely mutating into a social media form, and it was having dirty brutal intercourse with the lowest grade of pop 'culture'. I noticed that the colours were now increasingly fluorescent; while human lives were becoming increasingly blurry... before they began disappearing altogether in the distance... as they were decreasing in size and importance, as they were pushed further and further away... as it was becoming obvious that they were going to be gone, and disappear altogether... soon.

Modern European art was not dreaming about a 'better world'. It was hardly offering any social criticism.

But has it ever?

It was not calling people to the barricades... It was not dreaming about overthrowing the fascist global regime.

But after days in the Louvre and in the National Art Gallery, I was coming to a chilling realisation – it never has... Not in Europe... It was whoring here... For as long as we can remember, ever since we have been able to monitor...

Drunk, in fact totally stoned from an excessive intake of European classic and modern art, I struggled to remain firmly on the surface of our mother Earth.

The art was everywhere, all around me, and much of it was now absolutely free, here in Europe... But most of it was clearly on some sort of sinister mission – to simplify reality, to mute and humiliate all honest, positive and constructive emotions, to depoliticize societies, and in the end, to push people away from thinking and feeling altogether.

Perhaps it would have been better to have no art at all, than such art as this!

***

What was it that European propaganda was criticizing Soviet or Chinese art for? I recall words like 'censorship', and 'fear'!

The Louvre... Prado Museum... National Art Gallery... what else are those other than collections of incomparable and shameless orgies of submission, or servility, of cowardice, which would be inconceivable in any other culture on Earth?

Canvases of the Louvre: In horror, I observed the crawling infant Jesus depicted on every second painting... then crucifixions and of course countless resurrections... all with a frightening repetitiveness.

An image of baby Jesus with a perverse and adult face, crawling on the ground, while adults are watching with subservient admiration. There are images of some religious freaks with knives sticking out from their heads... There are bizarre angels flying, falling from the sky, fighting and threatening looking with their mean faces.

There are cardinals, bishops, and popes. And there are aristocrats, kings, governors and simply rich merchants who could afford to hire 'big artists'. All that creative prostitution; all those paintings produced to order, forming the essence of European culture; of European art!

I walked with my mother from hall to hall. "Great technique", she uttered sarcastically. Yes, I agreed, truly great technique... but the substance!

"All the might during those centuries was concentrated in the hands of the Church", commented my mother. "The Church was much more powerful than the throne and the aristocracy. And the church of course employed the greatest masters, such artists as Caravaggio, Leonardo da Vinci, and Rafael. And they were ready, happy, to be employed by the church, naturally, because the church paid them exquisitely, and because it was 'protecting them', making sure that they will not get burnt on the stake as so many others, and that they would not be tortured and murdered.... naturally, artists were not calling for rebellion, and there was no diversity of thought, no criticism of the system, or of the bestiality of the Christian dogma itself..."

In those years and centuries, Christianity murdered tens, hundreds of millions, of innocent people all over the world.

It financed 'expeditions' to what is now north and Latin America, to Africa, the Middle East, and to almost the whole of Asia.

Entire nations, countless great cultures were destroyed, and people of much more advanced civilizations, like the Inca, were forced to destroy their own identities, by ruining their own temples and dwellings, and then use the stones in order to erect monumental churches and cathedrals for the satisfaction of ruthless, merciless Christian invaders.

Where is all this being documented? Of course it can be seen in the great schools of painting: those of Peruvian Cusco and Ecuadorian Quito... but in the West?

Where in the Prado Museum in Madrid, are those sculptures and paintings depicting Christian barbarity? Where are those hundreds and thousands of artworks depicting Christian monstrosities: People being tortured for days and weeks, their bones broken on wheels, sharp objects inserted into their vaginas and rectums, men and women burnt on stakes? All this, so that they would admit that they are 'sinners', that they are 'evil'? That it is justifiable to murder them without remorse.

Where are those artists who would have dared to depict the results of the crusades – the bestiality, and the looting committed in the name of the cross? They are nowhere to be found – as they were all cozily copulating with the church, as they were paid by the church, and corrupted by the church!

Where are the paintings showing full Christian coffers, stretched from booty? And again, where are the images of the millions of victims, decapitated, cut to pieces, with their eyes poked out, tortured on stakes, burnt alive?

I walked slowly through the endless halls and corridors of French, Spanish, British and German museums. And I saw nothing, nothing at all, depicting crimes, genocides and holocausts committed by the most evil institution that ever existed on this earth; the most evil institution of all times – the Christian church.

This church, this horrific establishment which has been intimidating, scaring, and torturing billions of people worldwide, for millennia, is still 'morally' and 'intellectually' in control of the most powerful and the most destructive country on earth: the United States of America.

And it is still forming the cultural essence of Europe. It is – until now it still is!

In Europe, the majority of people may not go to churches, anymore, and it may not believe in Christian dogma… it may not believe in the religions at all, but its 'culture' is clearly shaped by aggressiveness, ruthlessness and the brutality of the Christian church and its realm.

It is not that 'people kidnapped good religion and made it monstrous' – it is religion that brainwashed people, entire nations, turning them into intolerant, bigoted murderers. But search for such thoughts on the canvases in the Louvre…

I saw almost no 'dissident' works in any of the major

museums of Europe.

I felt shame. And I felt horror at the monolithic essence of such spinelessness.

I was walked through the Louvre and through the National Gallery in London, blushing like a little boy.

How could this 'culture' criticize great artists in China or Russia, or Latin America? How could such a submissive and cowardly culture dare to criticize anything or anybody at all?

There, in Latin America and Asia, art has been standing tall; it has been at the vanguard of all changes, of progress!

Even in Indonesia, the greatest post-war painter is Djokopekik... My friend Djokopekik... An 'outrageous' political artist, with a fabulous heart on the left politically, with guts and endless courage... He used to be a former prisoner of conscience in the Western-backed jails of fascist, post-1965 Indonesia... A painter who immortalized Suharto as a swine, and former President – Megawati – as a puppet! And his own, brainwashed, indoctrinated nation, as a horde of monkeys!

Where are those 'brave' European 'masters'? Where are they, damn it!

Paintings, murals, posters, songs, theatre and cinema – they have all been struggling and attempting to improve societies in many parts of Asia and Latin America, even in Africa. How socially-oriented the greatest Latin American and Chinese art is! How empty, submissive, irrelevant, is art in the West!

In Venezuela, Brazil, in Ecuador and Bolivia, in Cuba, Chile and Nicaragua, art is offering both beauty and hope; it is searching for new directions for their societies. So many songs that are sang there are deep, poetic, with stunning lyrics and music. So many of them are 'engaged'.

***

The art in the West is now trying to cover up, by its complex curves and uneven squares, its total impotence, its moral emptiness, as well as the frightening brutality of European and North American culture.

As I walked through Paris, from the Sorbonne University to the Musee Quai Branly (the one that the French wanted to name, originally and arrogantly, as the "Museum of Primitive Arts"), I passed literally hundreds of art galleries.

In those days, the West had been, as I described in several of my recent essays, involved in a deliberate and determined attempt to destroy almost all the countries and governments that were still resisting its fascist grip on the global power.

'Opposition' movements were consistently manufactured in North America and Europe, and then implanted into Venezuela, China, Ukraine, Russia, Eritrea, Cuba, Bolivia, Brazil, and Zimbabwe, and to numerous other nations, on all continents. The Arab Spring has been literally derailed and bathed in blood, as the fascist and pro-Western military juntas have been arresting and murdering the opposition, and former revolutionaries.

I saw not one reflection of this reality in the galleries of Paris!

At one gallery I observed several metal dogs on long metal leashes that were sticking out into space... I was confronted by hundreds of pop topics, ranging from Italian sausages, nude girls and Frankenstein...

On Rue Mazarine, I was expected to admire several black garbage bags and one carton box... and then much the same in countless galleries of Quai Voltaire, only with more subdued and expensive finishing.

By now, France was heavily involved in almost all of its former African colonies. It has been playing as distractive a role on African continent, as the United States.

But you would never guess it from its visual art – from its museums and galleries!

It was all totally intellectually empty... It was finished... indifferent... and embarrassing. There were almost no dissident voices that were audible.

I was instinctively longing to escape from the Parisian art scene, as I, two days earlier, literally ran away from the National Gallery in London, 'cornered' by Juan de Valdez Leal and his "Immaculate Conception of the Virgin, with Two Donors", and the portrait of a pompous and obviously well paid Don Adrian Pulido Pareja, painted by Juan Bautista Martinez de Mazo.

I ran earlier, two years ago, from Brussels, where I kept stumbling over another 'great artwork' – statues of the King Leopold II, a true Belgian hero, who ordered the slaughter of a total of ten million Congolese people at the beginning of the 20th century – those who were accused of being too slow while working on his rubber plantation. The typical form of killing was the chopping off hands, but millions were also burnt alive, after being locked in their huts. Confronted by such deeds, one can hardly argue against the refinement and greatness of Christian and European culture!

Statues of Sir Winston Churchill and Lloyd George, those jolly good blokes who murdered millions of 'those niggers' in the Middle East and Africa, are also considered as masterpieces of European art, not to speak of the sculptures of dozens of the vile monsters responsible for genocides in the Americas – those that dot both Madrid and Lisbon. And there is no graffiti in Europe that would add at least some color to those gray and bronze 'masterpieces', like: "assassins!"

***

Frankly, ten days of hunting for meaningful European art exhausted and depressed me to the extreme.

I came there to search, once again, for truth, but I found centuries of accumulated propaganda, layer after layer – piling on top of each other.

This was perhaps my last attempt, as I had already spent years and decades studying Western art, crisscrossing Europe and North America, visiting museums, galleries, concert halls, opera houses, as well as all sorts of tunnels decorated by graffiti. It was time to accept the obvious conclusions, and to dedicate my time to something more meaningful.

I searched for kindness, but I found intimidation, fear, and brutality.

I searched for answers to all those horrors that were spread by the Western way of thinking... I found only pompous sculptures and canvases, repetitive and made to order.

There were some, very few, painters, like Otto Dix in Germany, or the Norwegian Munch. These two at least managed to show the tremendous fear that has been spread by Christianity, the hypocrisy and perversions of Western dogmas.

At Tate Modern, in London, there was a substantial exhibition of Soviet poster art. And at the Pompidou Center in Paris, I visited a huge and impressive exhibition of Henry Cartier-Bresson, which confirmed, once again, that one of the greatest photographers of all times was actually a Marxist and very close friend of both the Soviet Union and Communist China.

But these were clearly some exceptions, and most of them were like an echo from the past. It is a well known fact that Western art exploded out for three decades after the WWII, attempting to join humanity... Yes, it exploded, but it burned itself quickly, way too quickly! Emptiness and soullessness quickly returned.

As the world has been, once again, screaming in pain; as neo-colonialism has again been murdering tens of millions of men, women and children in Africa, Asia and the Middle East (but also in such places as Venezuela, Egypt and Ukraine), Western art continued to do what it did best, for centuries – painting absolute shit, and strictly to order.

Be it the church, the throne, the merchants or now the multi-national corporations or conservative governments – European and North American artists are ready to serve them all loyally, as long as there is an uninterrupted flow of dough! And they are ready to compete for this money, and to even cut each other throats.

They are eager, 'technically and artistically capable' to deliver anything that would stop progress, to cover up all those monstrous crimes of religion, business and the state. They are ready to turn their trade into a deadly weapon, to stir people away from conscience, from rational thinking, from compassion, even from love and from basic kind human instincts and feelings.

The fluorescent lights, and huge art installations filled with plastic straws and blinking lights for idiots – that is what it is all coming down to.

Billions of those who are starving to death and living in a gutter, matter nothing. They do not pay – therefore they do not exist.

7

UKRAINE: LIES AND REALITIES

Kiev.

Two beautiful Slavic sisters, Ukraine and Russia, pitched against each other: long hair flying in the wind, gray-blue eyes staring forward accusatively, but in the same time with anticipation and love.

One single moment, one wrong move, one word, and two countries, two allies, two almost identical cultures, can easily dash at each other's throats... Different words, different gestures, and they can also fall into each other's arms, instantly.

Is there going to be a war, a battle or an embrace? Is there going to be an insult or reconciliatory words?

Ironically, there is no 'self-grown dispute' between two nations. The seeds of mistrust, and possible tragedy, are sown by the outsiders, and nurtured by their malignant propaganda.

As Sergei Kirichuk, leader of progressive movement 'Borotba', explained:

"We have extensive invasion of western imperialism here. Imperialists were acting through huge network of NGOs and through the western-oriented politicians integrated into western establishment. Western diplomats declared that they invested more that 5 billions of dollars to 'development of democracy in Ukraine'. What kind of investment is it? How was this amount spent? We don't really know, but we can see the wide net of the US agents operating inside many key organizations and movements.

We can see that those 'western democracies' had not been concerned at all about growing of the far-right, Nazi movements. They had been ready to use the Nazis as a real armed force in overthrowing of Yanucovich.

President Yanucovich was actually totally pro-western politician, to start with. And his 'guilt' consisted only of his attempt to minimize the devastating aftermath that would come after implementation of the free trade zone with EU, on which the West was insisting."

***

Now Maidan, the main square of Kiev where the 'revolution' took place, is scarred, burned down, eerie.

Right-wingers, ultra-nationalists, young and not so young men with shaved heads, are watching pedestrians with confused, often provocative eyes.

Many of them are now controlling the traffic and, like in Thailand where the right-wingers also recently 'protested, are deciding who can pass and who cannot. The law is clearly and patently in their hands, or more precisely, in Maidan area, they are the law.

Religious symbols are suddenly everywhere, while monuments to heroes of the revolution and the WWII are desecrated.

At the makeshift stage used by right-wing extremists, there is a huge crucifixion as well as Virgin Marry.

But many right-wingers are at total disarray, they are outraged, as one of their leaders, Aleksandr Muzychko, was murdered just one day earlier.

Oleh Odnorozhenko is speaking. He is angry, irritated, accusing the state, the same government his people brought to power through the coup just a short time ago, of political murder. He is calling for 'the second stage of the revolution', as if one past stage would not be terrible enough, already.

My friend Alexander is explaining to me: "This is going to be a tremendous mess. The West used all fascist and ultra-nationalist forces to destroy legitimate government of Ukraine, but paradoxically, these ultra right-wingers are essentially against both NATO and all those agreements with the European Union."

Afghanistan, Al-Qaida, scenario, in brief and on smaller scale: use any force, any radicals, as long as you can manage to destroy the Soviet Union and later, Russia.

"They are going to get into each other's hair very soon", predicts Alexandr, former military intelligence officer.

***

The car is negotiating a bumpy four-lane highway between Kiev and Odessa. There are three of us on board – my translator, Dimitry from the Liva.com site, a driver, and me. Having left Kiev in the morning, we are literally flying at 160km/h towards Odessa.

The wide fields of Ukraine, formerly known as the 'breadbasket' of the Soviet Union, look depressingly unkempt. Some are burnt.

"What are they growing here?" I ask.

Nobody knows, but both of my friends agree that almost everything in Ukraine is now collapsing, after the decomposition of the USSR, and this includes both industry and agriculture. The roads are not an exception, either.

"They only built facades during the last decades", explains Dimitry. "The core, the essence had been constructed in the Soviet era. And now everything is crumbling."

***

I have no idea where the official numbers come from; those

81

that say that Ukraine is evenly divided between those who support the West, and those who feel their identity is closely linked with Russia. Maybe this might be the case in Western Ukraine, in Lvov, or even in the capital – Kiev. But Western Ukraine has only a few key cities. The majority of people in this country of around forty-four million are concentrated in the south, east and southeast, around the enormous industrial and mining centers of Donetsk, Dnepropetrovsk, and Krivoi Rog. There is Odessa in the south, and Kharkov 'the second capital' in the east. And people in all those parts of the country mainly speak Russian. And they see, what has recently happened in Kiev as an unceremonious coup, orchestrated and supported by the West.

***

Before reaching Odessa we leave the highway and drive northeast, towards Moldova and its small separatist enclave, called Transnistria.

There, the river Kuchurgan separates the Ukrainian town of Kuchurgan and the Transnistrian city of Pervomaisc.

I see no Russian tanks at Pervomaisc, no artillery. There is absolutely no military movement whatsoever, despite the countless Western mass media reports testifying (in abstract terms) to the contrary.

I cross the bridge on foot and ask the Transnistrian border guard, whether he has recently seen any foreign correspondents arriving from the United States or the European Union, attempting to cross the border and verify the facts. He gives me a bewildered look.

I watch beautiful white birds resting on the surface of the river, and then I return to Ukraine.

There, two ladies who run the 'Camelot Bar' served us the most delicious Russo/Ukrainian feast of an enormous borscht soup, and pelmeni.

Russian television station blasts away, and the two women

cannot stop talking; they are frank, proud, and fearless. I turn on my film camera, but they don't mind:

"Look what is happening in Kiev", exclaims Alexandra Tsyganskaya, the owner of the restaurant. "The US and the West were planning this; preparing this, for months, perhaps years! Now people in Ukraine are so scared, most of them are only whispering. They are petrified. There is such tension everywhere, that all it would take is to light a match and everything will explode."

Her friend, Evgenia Chernova, agrees: "In Odessa, Russian-speaking people get arrested, and they are taken all the way to Kiev. The same is happening in Kharkov, in Donetsk, and elsewhere. They call it freedom of speech! All Russian television channels are banned. What you see here is broadcasted from across the border. They treat people like cattle. But our people are not used to this: they will rebel, they will resist! And if they push them to the edge, it will be terrible!"

Both women definitely agree on one thing: "We say, 'don't provoke Russia!' It is a great nation, our historical ally. It has been helping us for decades."

'A civil war', I hear in Kuchurgan. 'A civil war!' I hear in Odessa. 'A civil war!' I hear in Kharkov.

And the same words in Odessa are even written on huge banners: "Kiev, people are not cattle!"

Odessa city, that architectural jewel, an enormous southern port, is now relatively quiet, but tense. I speak to the manager of the historic and magnificently restored Hotel Bristol, but she is very careful in choosing her words. I mention Western involvement in the coup, or in the 'revolution' as many in Kiev and in the West call it, but she simply nods, neutrally.

I cross the street and enter the Odessa Philharmonic Theatre. A young lady approaches me: "Would you like to have my ticket?" She asks in perfect Russian. "My boyfriend did not show up. Please enjoy."

The performance is bizarre, and clearly 'un-philharmonic'. Some renowned folk ensemble performs old Ukrainian traditional songs and dances, but why here and why now? Is it a patriotic gesture, or something else?

The city is subdued, as well as those famous Potemkin Stairs: Renowned for one of the most memorable scenes in world cinema that of, the silent film 'Battleship Potemkin' directed in 1925 by Sergei M. Eisenstein.

As Helen Grace once wrote:

The Odessa steps massacre in the film condenses the suppression, which actually occurred in the city, into one dramatised incident, and this remains one of the most powerful images of political violence ever realised.

One only hopes that Odessa never again falls victim to unbridled political cruelty, such as was visited on the people by the feudal, oppressive right-wing Tsarist regime, at the beginning of the 20th century!

***

Babushka looks exhausted and subdued. She is slowly digging into dark earth, all alone, clearly abandoned.

I spotted some collapsed houses in the village that we had passed just a few minutes earlier, and I asked the driver to make a U-turn, but he clearly did not see any urgency and continued to drive on: "You will see many villages like this", he explained. Dimitry confirmed: "Such villages one are all over Ukraine. There are thousands of them; literally, you see them whenever you leave the main roads."

This one, this village, is called Efremovka, and the name of a grandmother is Lyubov Mikhailovna.

We are somewhere between the cities of Nikolayev and Krivoi Rog.

All around us are the ruins of agricultural estates, of small factories, and houses that used to belong to farmers. Wires are missing from electric poles, and everything appears to be static, like in a horror science-fiction film. Only Lyubov Mikhailovna is digging, stubbornly.

I ask her how she is managing to survive, and she replies

that she is not managing at all.

"How could one survive here on only one thousand Hryvnas per month (around US$80)?" she laments. "We are enduring only on what we grow here: cucumbers, tomatoes, potatoes..."

I ask her about the ruins of houses, all around this area, and she nods for a while, and only then begins speaking: "People abandoned their homes and their villages, because there are no jobs. After the Soviet Union collapsed, the entire Ukraine has been falling apart... People are leaving and they are dying. Young people try to go abroad.... The government is not even supplying us with gas and drinking water, anymore. We have to use the local well, but the water is contaminated by fertilizers – it is not clean..."

"Was it better before?" I ask.

Her face brightens up. She stops speaking for a while, searching her memory, recalling long bygone days. Then she answers: "How can you even ask? During the Soviet Union everything was better, much better! We all had jobs and there were decent salaries, pensions... We had all that we needed."

Looking around me, I quickly recall that Ukraine is an absolute demographic disaster: even according to official statistics and censuses, the number of people living in this country fell from 48,457,102 in 2001 to 44,573,205 in 2013. Years after its 'independence', and especially those between 1999 and 2001, are often described as one of the worst demographic crises in modern world history. In 1991 the population of Ukraine was over 51.6 million!

Only those countries that are devastated by brutal civil wars are experiencing similar population decline.

***

Krivoi Rog or Kryvyi Rih as it is known in the Ukrainian language – is arguably the most important steel manufacturing city in Eastern Europe, and a large globally important, metallurgical center for what is known as the Kryvbas iron- ore mining region.

Here Krivorozhstal, one of the most important steel factories in the world, it had seen outrageous corruption scandals during its first wave of privatization. During the second privatization in 2005, the mammoth factory was taken over by the Indian multi-national giant, Mittal Steel (which paidUS$4.81 billion), and was renamed Arcelor Mittal Kryvyi Rih. Since then, production has declined significantly, and thousands of workers were unceremoniously fired.

According to the Arcelor Mittal Factbooks (2007 and 2008), steel production decreased from 8.1 million tons in 2007, to 6.2 million tones in 2008. In 2011, the workforce decreased from 55,000 to 37,000 tons, and the management is still hoping that even more dramatic job cuts (down to 15,000) can be negotiated.

By late afternoon, we arrived at the main gate of the factory. Hundreds of people were walking by; most of them looking exhausted, discouraged and unwilling to engage in any conversation.

Some shouted anti-coup slogans, but did not want to give their names or go on the record.

Finally, a group of tough looking steelworkers stops, and begins to discuss the situation at the factory with us, passionately:

"Do you realize how little we earn here? People at this plant, depending on their rank, bring home only some US$180, US$260, or at most some US$450 a month. Across the border, in Russia, in the city of Chelyabinsk, the salaries are three to four times higher!"

His friend is totally wound up and he screams: "We are ready! We will go! People are reaching the limit!"

It is hard to get any political sense from the group, but it is clear that opinions are divided: while some want more foreign investment, others are demanding immediate nationalization. They have absolutely no disputes with Russia, but some support the coup in Kiev, while others are against it.

It is clear that, more than ideology; these people want some practical improvement in their own lives and in the life of their city.

"All we have heard, for the past twenty years is that things will improve", explains the first steel worker. "But look what is happening in reality. Mittal periodically fails to pay what is due. For instance, I am supposed to get 5,700 Hryvnas a month, but I get less than 5,000. And the technology at the plant is old, outdated. The profits that Mittal is making – at least if some of it would stay here, in Ukraine, and go to the building of the roads or improving the water supplies... But they take everything out of the country."

The next day, in Kharkov, Sergei Kirichuk, concludes:

"People all over the world are fighting against so-called 'free market', but in Ukraine, to bring it here, was the main reason for the 'revolution'. It is really hard to believe."

***

The border between Ukraine and Russia, near the town of Zhuravlevka, between Ukrainian Kharkov and the Russian city of Belgorod, is quiet. Good weather, wide fields and an almost flat landscape, guarantee good visibility for several kilometers. On the 28 of March, when Western and Ukrainian mass media were shouting about an enormous Russian military force right at the border, I only saw a few frustrated birds and an apparently unmanned watch tower.

The traffic at the border was light, but it was flowing – and several passenger cars were crossing from the Russian side to Ukraine.

What I saw, however, were several Ukrainian tanks along the M-20/E-105 highway, just a stone throw away from the borderline. There were tanks and there were armored vehicles, and quite a substantial movement of Ukrainian soldiers.

The local press was, however, not as aggressive, provocative:

"State of War!" shouted the headlines of Kyiv Post. "We lifted up to the sky 100 jet fighters, in order to scare Moscow", declared 'Today'.

***

The reality on the ground differed sharply from the 'fairytales', paid for and propagated by Western mass media outlets and by the 'free Ukrainian press'.

In Kharkov, Soviet banners flew in the wind, next to many Russian flags. Thousands of people gathered in front of the giant statue of Lenin on those windy days of 28th and 29th of March.

There were fiery speeches and ovations. The outraged crowd met the proclamations that the Western powers had instigated the 'fascist coup' in Kiev, with loud shouts: "Russia, Russia!"

Old women, Communist leaders, and my friend Sergei Kirichuk, as well as people from international solidarity organizations, made fiery speeches. Apparently, the government in Kiev had already begun to cut the few social benefits that were left, including free medical assistance. Several hospitals were poised to close down, soon.

People were ready to fight; to defend themselves against those hated neo-liberal policies, for which (or against which) none of them had been allowed to vote for.

"In Crimea, people voted, overwhelmingly, to return to Russia", explained a young man, a student, Alexei. "But the West calls it unconstitutional and undemocratic. In Ukraine itself, the democratically elected government has been overthrown and policies that nobody really wants are being pushed down our throats. And… this is called democracy!"

In an apartment of the Borodba movement, a young leader and history student, Irina Drazman, spoke about the way the West destroyed Ukraine. She reminded me of a Chilean student leader and now an MP – Ms. Camila Vallejo. Irina is only twenty, but coherent and as sharp as a razor.

"There is great nostalgia for the Soviet Union", she explains. "If only it could be re-shaped and the concept improved, most of the people in Ukraine would be happy to be part of it again."

And that is exactly what the West tries to prevent: A powerful and united country, one which can defend the interest of its people.

Standing in front of a police cordon in Kharkov, Alexandr Oleinik, a Ukrainian political analyst, explains:

"The essence of what is now happening is based on the doctrine of the United States, which has one major goal: To wipe out from the globe, first the Soviet Union, and then Russia, regardless of its form; whether socialist or capitalist... As is well known, these goals were already defined in the early 1980's, by Zbigniew Brzezinski, in his report to the US Department of State, "Game Plan: A Geostrategic Framework for the Conduct of the U.S.-Soviet Contest".

Besieged square in front of the court of justice may not be the most comfortable place for political discussions, but Mr. Oleinik has plenty to share:

"After destroying USSR, the US is, until now, making enormous effort to, in accordance with the 'Brzezinski Doctrine', to drag Russia, Ukraine and other post-Soviet countries, into exhausting regional conflicts, in order to out root from the consciousness of the people of these nations all thoughts about reunification (be it a customs union, common economic sphere, etc.). Series of 'color revolutions' from so-called American doctrine of 'advancement of democracies' became a clear proof of the essence of the geopolitical interests of the US. Libya, Tunis, Egypt, Iraq, Afghanistan, Syria, and Yugoslavia – all this is from the same shelf."

"Venezuela, Cuba, Bolivia, Ecuador, Zimbabwe, Eritrea, even China", I continue.

Policemen are looking at us suspiciously, as both of us are naming dozens and dozens of countries located in all corners of the world.

***

In Kiev's Maidan, the main square where the 'revolution' or the coup took place, the right-wing groupings are hanging around, aimlessly. Some men and women are frustrated. Many now even feel that they were fooled.

Thousands were paid to participate in what was thought would bring at least some social justice, some relief. But the interim government began taking dictate, almost immediately: from the United States, from European Union and from the institutions such as IMF and World Bank.

Now thousands of disgruntled 'revolutionaries' feel frustrated. Instead of saving the country, they sold all ideals, and betrayed their own people. And their own lives went from bad to worse.

The tension is growing and Ukraine is on the edge.

There is growing tension, even confrontation, between conservative, oppressive forces and those progressive ones. There is tension between Russian speakers and those who are insisting on purely Ukrainian language being used all over the country.

There are political assassinations; there is fear and uncertainty about the future.

There is increasing and negative role being played by the religions: from Protestant to Orthodox.

Nobody knows what will follow the coup. Confusion and frustration, as well as social collapse, may well cause a brutal civil war.

Protesters are now, this very moment, occupying government buildings in Donetsk and Lugansk, demanding referendum. Majority of people in these and other cities would rather join Russia then to live in pro-Western dictatorship, which Ukraine became after the coup.

Same tactics that were lauded by Western propaganda during the Maidan uprising are now hypocritically condemned in the east and south of the country.

Russia gained greatly, especially in the non-Western world. It is now recognized as the center of global 'mutiny' against global dictatorship of the US and EU. It opened one more front of resistance, and it stands alongside countries of Latin America.

Its generally peaceful and measured approach is in direct contrast to brutal and destabilizing methods used by the US and EU all over the globe. Except in those few fully indoctrinated modern-day colonies (which the West calls 'democracies' just because the people there can stick a piece of paper to a carton box, and most are stupidly doing so), the world is waking up to reality that there actually is, suddenly, some strong and determined resistance to Western imperialism.

After decades of total darkness, the hope is emerging.

In the meantime, two beautiful Slavic countries are still facing each other. But the people, particularly those in Ukraine, are now waving Russian flags and shout to the faces of riot police that is obedient to Kiev: "Russia! Russia!"

No matter what the propaganda says, reality is well known. For decades, after destruction of the USSR, Ukraine mainly obeyed the West and Russia went its own, determinedly independent way.

The result is: Ukraine is on its knees (although not as horribly yet as some East European countries like Bulgaria, that actually became full members of the EU). Wages for workers and pensions for elderly are now approximately 3-4 times higher in Russia than in Ukraine.

And Russia has its own, independent voice, flying all over the world though the outlets like RT and Voice of Russia, while Ukraine is a clearly a colony.

It is obvious in what direction the majority of Ukrainians is now looking with hope. The government should listen. It should also call referendum, soon. It should use 'direct democracy', not some rigged multi-party charade like in Indonesia.

Two countries that share both history and the future, should embrace. And face the wind, and tremors, together! They should never fight each other – Russia and Ukraine are soul mates, not enemies. Those who are dividing them should be exposed, shamed, and expelled!

Andre Vltchek

8

CHRISTIANITY,
GUILTY AS CHARGED!

Motto: verse from Colossians 3:22: "Slaves, obey your masters."

It is Easter and I am mourning for all those hundreds of millions, perhaps billions, who were forced to 'die for Jesus'... They vanished so the Christian dogma of some crucified man from Nazareth, could be lubricated and substantiated with red oceans of human blood, and reinforced with a tremendous mountain of bones. Colossal flames have burnt countless millions of those who have found this entirely psychedelic tale, thoroughly unbelievable, even ridiculous.

Nobody asked Jesus to die for this world, or to wash away all of its 'sins' (always, always those 'sins'!). But hundreds of millions had to vanish to give way for those 'following him'; who held their crosses while cutting down people with their swords!

"In the name of the cross!" "In the name of Jesus!" Slaughter and torture, burnt flesh, mutilated bodies, beastly rapes. The history of this world, Mr. Fukuyama! It is mainly a history of Christian conquests, the enslavement of the planet, and murder in the name of the cross. Is it over; is it the end of such a history, really?

***

Today I want to remember, to mourn, those centuries of human sacrifice. That pointless, unnecessary, vile human sacrifice!

I want to commemorate those who have vanished; I want to do it with with red wine. Not with the wine that symbolizes 'blood' of someone, but with the wine of the Chilean people who produced it. As simple as that!

And I want to ask one simple but urgent question: "Isn't it time to stop, to say enough? Isn't it time to scrap that more than 2,000 years old violent dogma, which is most definitely responsible for the insanity, and for the arrangement of world as it today?"

On Saturday and Sunday, believers and non-believers will be packing tens of thousands of churches in North America and Europe, in Latin America, Africa, Oceania, and even in some parts of Asia. For many, this 'celebration' has nothing to do with god, or God, or any philosophical, even spiritual concept. For many, maybe for the majority of the patrons, this is just a habit, a custom, or something much more sinister: The reinforcement of a sense of belonging to something that they are told (or hinted to), is the right direction on the highway to righteousness and superiority.

***

Religions, most of them, are actually like some sort of huge private club with inflexible rules, rigidly defined membership guidelines, and fees.

Except that, while you can be kicked out from the club, religions can actually kill... and they do – which is especially true of Christianity.

Those who are gathering during these days, and celebrating the resurrection of an individual they call Jesus, are clearly overlooking, and even forgetting the price, which humanity has been paying, all over the world, for millennia. For just a single crucifixion and for the short agony of one person (who perhaps never even existed), entire nations were placed on the sacrificial altar.

How primitive and brutal, and how immoral!

Almost the entire North and South America, in the era of the arrival of the priests, shuttled to the "New World" by that arch criminal Christopher Columbus (Colon) and his fleet, got ruined, massacred, cheated and contaminated by all sorts of diseases. The Cross – the symbol of Christianity – was always at the front and above all that carnage. There was really 'no coming back' for the conquerors. Those holding the cross were too intoxicated by vile righteousness; they were too overwhelmed by greed, too sadistic.

Unbridled greed, religious fanaticism and oppressed sexuality (those very pillars of Christianity) played the most terrifying role in ruining this, (and many other) parts of the world.

The great majority of people from the so-called New World simply vanished.

"When Columbus landed in this hemisphere, there were probably 80-100 million people with advanced civilizations: Commerce, cities, etc. Not long afterwards about 95% of this population had disappeared", explained Noam Chomsky, during our conversation, which led to our book "On Western Terrorism, From Hiroshima to Drone Warfare".

Those who were not killed were brutalized savagely.

Abel Posse, a great Argentinean writer and diplomat, the author of the novel "Dogs of Paradise" ("Los perros del paraíso"), once wrote and also explained to me personally:

"The conquest was sick... And religious 'guilt' played a tremendous role in the violence. Local women were willing to engage in sexual acts with those pathetic conquerors who wore crosses and heavy armor in the tropical heat... And the conquerors were possessed by desire... but also by terrible guilt. They saw the willingness and desire of the local women as a sin... Therefore, they dragged those beautiful women into deep forests, tortured them for hours and days, and then raped them brutally!"

Whoever survived was forcefully converted to Christianity.

Both sexual torture (for which 'ingenious' instruments were invented and manufactured) and rape were not the only types of violence administered by 'pious' Christians, but they were the most common ones, for which they are remembered, until now, in Peru and elsewhere.

In the era of conquest, the much more advanced culture of South and Central America was ruined, people were captured and enslaved. Their languages were banned or made irrelevant.

Men and women were forced to take apart, stone by stone, their tremendous temples, and then build cathedrals and churches. Then, these Christian temples of worship were decorated with looted gold and silver, extracted by de facto slaves, chained in appalling mines around places like Potosi. This was what the great Uruguayan writer, Eduardo Galeano, described as the "Open Veins of Latin America".

And slavery was, of course, always one of the trademarks of the Christian conquerors. And the Bible itself was conveniently quoted buy those beasts clad in metal armor and huge crosses: "Slaves, obey your masters."

Entire continents and whole nations were enslaved. Proud people, who used to be free and proud, were chained. They were hunted like animals, by European Christians and then taken by the millions in order to build, for free, the 'new continents' (millions died on high seas)... The Brits and French pioneered this horrid practice, but there were many others, including Belgians and Germans.

As was honestly confirmed by R. Furman, a Baptist, of South Carolina: "The right of holding slaves is clearly established in the Holy Scriptures, both by precept and example."

The Church, particularly the Vatican, but not alone, financed (and 'invested in') those countless crusades and colonial expeditions. Its approach towards the world was greedy, ruthless, and murderous, or more precisely, genocidal.

Absolutely no religion on earth has ever managed to achieve such preposterous levels of brutality with such disregard and spite for fellow human beings, such racism and bigotry.

At one point, the Spanish aristocracy was so appalled with Christianity, that it sent its ships to Africa, and begged Muslim armies standing in Ceuta, to liberate Spain from Christian terror. Which happened, and Muslims established, among other oases of tolerance and calm, the Caliphate of Cordoba, where in a tremendous mosque, Christians, Jews and Muslims were allowed to gather, pray and openly discuss almost any topic they desired.

To illustrate the contrast, "One of the mottos of the first European migrants to what is now New England, was 'Convert or Die!'" explained a Czech/American artist and filmmaker from Boston, Milan Kohout.

***

Based on facts that are readily available to any person who is willing to study and read, Christianity should be banned. The ban should be simply based on the countless crimes against humanity, which have, by hundred-fold exceeded even those crimes committed by Nazism (Christianity and Fascism/Nazism are actually very closely connected).

No dogma, no ideology, has enslaved the world, like Christianity. No religion or ideology has murdered more people.

The only reason why it has not happened yet, is because Christianity is actually still clearly in charge of the world order; its 'culture' is the dominant philosophy of Empire, and its self-righteousness is almost never allowed to be openly questioned in the mass media.

In ancient eras and in modern times, Christianity has been deeply and negatively involved in almost all the chapters of history, in the most despicable manner.

It came out in full support of colonialism, slavery and racism, and then it collaborated with, and endorsed Nazism in Germany, Mussolini's fascism in Italy, General Franco in Spain, and the 'fight against Communism' in Eastern Europe.

Adolf Hitler was inspired by Christianity, and by its hate for everything from secularism to Communism, from 'pornography' to homosexuality.

In 1936 he declared: "Providence withdrew its protection and our people fell... And in this hour we sink to our knees and beseech our almighty God that He may bless us, that He may give us the strength to carry on the struggle for the freedom, the future, the honor, and the peace of our people. So help us God."

He had it all very clear two years earlier:

"National Socialism neither opposes the Church nor is it anti-religious, but on the contrary it stands on the ground of a real Christianity... For their interests cannot fail to coincide with ours alike in our fight against the symptoms of degeneracy in the world of today, in our fight against a Bolshevist culture, against an atheistic movement, against criminality, and in our struggle for a consciousness of a community in our national life...These are Christian principles!"

And of course, a part of Christianity has always been 'charity'. After massacring millions of innocent men, women and children, or after robbing entire nations of all that they possessed, the Christians happily gave back. If it took 90%, it gave 10%, or much less than 1% (in case of the United States, when it comes to foreign aid). Again, to quote Adolf Hitler, a Christian:

"With a tenth of our budget for religion, we would thus have a Church devoted to the State and of unshakable loyalty."

Even before Hitler, those German genocides against the Herero and Nama tribes in and around of what is now

Namibia, came with the clear blessing of the clergy.

Perhaps in the most intense genocide of the 20th Century, the rule of the Belgian King Leopold II took approximately ten million lives, or roughly half of the population of the "Congo Free State", according to investigations by the anthropologist Jan Vansina and others. After his death, King Leopold II was interred in the royal vault at the Church of Our Lady of Laeken, in Brussels.

No wonder the King supposedly argued "bringing Christianity to the country outweighs a little starvation..." Ten million people mutilated and burnt alive is clearly nothing too scandalous for Christian sensitivities, as long as it helped to spread true teaching to those 'barbarians', in the 'heart of darkness'.

Of course, most of the Latin American dictators were deeply religious and 'moral', including General Pinochet, who reigned brutally with the determined support of the United States, Opus Dei, and other extremist Christian clans.

In Argentina, Christianity was one of the pillars and justifications of the terror administered by Jorge Rafael Videla and his military junta. He used to say: "We consider it a great crime to work against the Western and Christian style of life: It is not just the bomber but the ideologist who is the danger." He also periodically clarified his deep and compassionate inclinations: "As many people as necessary must die in Argentina so that the country will again be secure."

One of the most brutal men of the 20th century, Francois 'doc' Duvalier, went even one step further, and declared that he is part of God and Jesus Crist. His posters used to declare: "Papa Doc: One with... Jesus Christ and God himself".

The Western Christian demagogues and propagandists implanted a fear of secularism and atheism, to many regions of the world, with mostly horrifying results: Jihadist cadres were financed and introduced into Afghanistan during the war with the Soviet Union. The 1965 US-backed military coup in Indonesia which took between one and three million lives (mainly atheists and secular intellectuals, murdered by the military, Muslim cadres, but with the clear involvement of other religions) was one of the most horrific orgies of terror from which Indonesia has never recovered, and gradually degenerated into a religious and thoroughly unproductive, ignorant archipelago of environmentally plundered and devastated islands. The British Empire used the "divide and rule" strategy, which led to the awful 'Partition' of the sub-Continent.

And this is just to name few of the deadliest religious implants, orchestrated by the Christian West.

***

In today's world, Christians are siding with the most appalling regimes, supporting the most dreadful oppressions.

I spoke to several priests and believers in Cairo, not long after the brutal pro-Western military coup of al-Sisi and his clique, which, on July 3rd 2013, overthrew the democratically elected moderate Islamic government. All of them were staunch supporters of the coup d'état that killed several thousand people in just a few weeks.

Even Time admitted: For Egypt's 8 million Christians... the coup seemed little short of a miracle. Some hailed al-Sisi as a messiah...

In Africa, most of the extreme violence has religious, Christian connotations. In the Democratic Republic of Congo, which has lost, since 1995, between six and ten million people, some of the most brutal militias fall into the bracket of Christian fundamentalists.

A close ally of the West and one of the most brutal dictators in Africa, Yoweri Museveni, responsible for millions of lost lives in the Democratic Republic of Congo and in his native Uganda, and a self-proclaimed crusader against homosexuality, has been for decades, a staunch Christian and is associated with the American fundamentalist Christian organization, "The Fellowship" (also known as "The Family").

And there is, of course, The Lord's Resistance Army,

originally from Uganda, but operating in the entire region. It uses child soldiers; it has been accused of committing numerous crimes against humanity; "including massacres, abductions, mutilation, torture, rape, and uses forced child labor as soldiers, porters, and sex slaves". Its commander, Joseph Kony, proclaims himself the spokesperson of God and a spirit medium, primarily of the "Holy Spirit".

One of the most brutal actors in the Congolese genocide, former warlord Laurent Nkunda, is an ordained Christian preacher and an ordained minister. Most of his troops had been followers (not that they had much choice). His men are responsible for some of the most horrible crimes in modern history, including mass rapes in the city of Bukavu. The Motto of his militia is: "Rebels for Christ." He is a Seventh-day Adventist. He also claims to receive help and guidance from American "Rebels for Christ" who visit the Congo spreading Pentecostal Christianity.

Christianity still plays some of the most negative roles in both Africa and Oceania (Polynesia, Melanesia and Micronesia), where it is responsible for the physical (mostly sexual) and mental abuse of both children and adults, for defending oppressive family structures and the status quo in the society, as well as for spreading disinformation and ignorance. It is also extracting funds from the congregation, rich and poor, financially ruining its members.

Outrageous financial extractions are also common in countries such as the Philippines, as well as in several Christian pockets of Indonesia, where Christianity is corrupt to the extreme, siding, for decades, with the most extreme 'free-market' dogma, and heartless business practices. There, it actually forms the 'Fifth Column' – it is helping to plunder the country on behalf of foreign companies – mostly those that, of course, come from the Christian West.

It goes without saying that places that have recently undergone pro-Western and 'anti-people' 'reforms' and 'uprisings', are witnessing increasing religious, often Christian zeal, most cases implanted and supported from abroad. This is true of Ukraine, Cuba, Venezuela, to name just a few.

The Ukrainian fascists, who overthrew the elected government in Kiev, are now giving speeches in Maidan Square, surrounded by huge crucifixes and a statue of the Virgin Mary. Both the Orthodox Church and Protestants (I was told that the present leaders explained that true global power is in the hands of Western Protestants, which resulted in quick conversions) are gaining power.

But the Empire is the one that performs most of the crimes against humanity. These crimes are habitually committed in the name of Christianity.

That very Empire is mainly governed by deeply religious, dedicated Christians, mostly Protestant (all 41 Presidents of the United States have been Protestants, except for J.F. Kennedy, who was a Roman Catholic).

'Exceptionalism', is a deep belief that the West has been given some sort of mandate "from above" to govern, judge and police the world – it all comes from the fundamentalist Christian faith.

Coming back full circle to the original point that this essay is making, almost all the horrors this planet has experienced, actually come from that intolerant, racist and 'exceptionalism' belief, clearly propelled by Christian faith, and by, other less influential, monotheist religions.

This belief is encoded in Christianity and in the Bible, and has been put to work by all the generations and almost all Christian theoreticians. It is not, as so many naïve people say: That bad people kidnapped an excellent idea and faith.

According to this belief, nothing really matters much, as long as the ruling Christian culture stays in power, as long as the Christian West continues to rule over the world. As in the middle ages, no human sacrifice is high enough, as long as the system is upheld. As long as the victims are 'the others' – Arabs, Jews, Southeast Asians, Chinese, Pacific Islanders, Chinese or Japanese (and the system uses collaborators from the ranks of these ethnic groups, as well. The carrot consists of; making them think, that by serving the West through

Christian religion and business, they are actually gaining an exclusive status, that of local 'elites').

The sacrifice of 'the others' is expected, even welcomed: Seven or even ten million people in Indochina – not a big deal. Three million in Indonesia – it is irrelevant. Ten million in Congo – who cares, they are Christians, but in reality some second rate niggers, just to borrow the vocabulary of the British Christian Prime Minister Lloyd George. Tens of millions all over Africa, from Somalia to Mali – who are they? Un-people, just filthy Muslims! Millions of broken lives all over Latin America – good for them! They were mainly Communists, and atheist hordes. Twenty million Soviet people died fighting and defeating Nazism – they were mainly white, but their atheism made them worse than those niggers!

Christian 'logic' was clearly implemented in all the colonialist adventures and genocides of modern days; in Iraq, Afghanistan, and Libya, to name just a few.

As has always been reflected by the 'Monroe Doctrine' – the US has the right to determine the fate of people and nations all over Latin America.

Such a belief has also been easily detectable in all former and present colonialist expansions, in the slave trade, and in the extermination of entire nations. As is evident in how the West is treating two enormous nations: China and Russia.

Many analysts and thinkers were naively waiting for some glimpse of real logic, based on facts, morality, and international law… They waited in vain. The Empire acted religiously. The Empire IS religious! It demanded total obedience and faith. It was ready to burn millions of those who were prepared to resist- even question – metaphorically and in real terms.

That is, naturally, nothing new! Many have noticed that the West is in fact a fundamentalist Christian entity. Its people are mainly secular (except in the United States, the most religious industrialized country on earth) – they don't care much about practical religious aspects, about visiting churches or about symbolism. But their brains, minds and tolerance to the brutality committed by their societies, are conditioned by

Christian dogmas and by the 'theories of exclusiveness', by the profound belief that they, and only they, have the right to hold the fate of this planet in their hands.

***

On one of the many Internet sites dedicated to the crimes committed by Christianity, young people mainly, are compiling the list. In simple terms, saying the same thing that is being argued in this essay.

"Mental and Physical abuse of children", writes one.

"Ignorance", jumps in another writer.

"...Mental abuse of children and adult alike, murder, torture, sexual abuse of children and adult alike, several hundred years of stupidity and the humiliation of other nations and ethnicities (including the slavery of Africa and the creation of the idea that "black is inferior"), actual killing and righteousness... for degrading black people, homosexuals and Jews... demonizing people for being an individual with critical thinking..."

"The crusades..."

"The delusions, fears and wasted lives of billions of followers."

"Remember the crusades? There was a children's crusade. It was pretty nasty. Christianity never had a problem with killing babies in the name of their vicious god. That's why it's so ironic that they're always screaming about being 'pro life'."

"Those nasty pretend nice women who maltreat everyone else who is not like them, and teach their children to do the same."

And so on. The list of grievances is endless.

***

The Last Supper, which is one of the main symbols of Christianity, has most certainly been relived worldwide, in the countries battered by the Western ideological dogma, based on the Christian views of the world.

But those millions, who were metaphorically crucified (they most often died a much worse death than that caused by crucifixion), were not sons or daughters of a god or the God; destined to be resurrected at a later date. They were simple men and women who were taken to terrible prisons or camps, in order to be exterminated... or simply shot to death like stray dogs. They were raped and then cut to pieces, they had heart attacks and strokes from electric shocks, they had their bones crushed, and they were burnt by cigarettes, and often, later, burnt to death, alive.

They were resistance fighters struggling against Christian-backed dictatorships in Chile, Argentina, the Dominican Republic, Kenya, and so many other unfortunate corners of the globe. Or they were simply free-minded men and women, unwilling to live those dreadful lives, under Christian hypocrisy and its dismal dictates.

They had their last meals with their loved ones, before the bell rang, before the door was kicked open, before they were taken away, before they were never resurrected, before they never returned home.

I propose a toast, to those hundreds of millions of victims of Christian terror. And especially to the millions of those who resisted it, and died with honor and great dignity, fighting for humanity!

I salute the men and women of the Western Hemisphere who fought the European invaders; those who have always come armed with their deadly weapons, crosses, and terrifying visions of total doom, and hell.

Claiming that it brings love, Christianity offers fear and suffering to the planet. Enough! Truly, enough!

They advise us to offer our other cheek? Yes, they do. OUR cheek, of course, not theirs. If you slap them, they will machine gun you down, blow you to pieces. If they come and rape your children in front of you, as they have been doing for centuries, you are supposed to serve them dinner, afterwards.

Their charity, too! It is like their foreign aid. Loot

everything, and then give 0.02%!

And their last, and final dogma: "It is not really religion, which is bad. It is the 'people' who kidnapped it."

This is the worst, the wildest lie – the most predictable, the cheapest, and the most insulting of lies. Insulting to logic, and insulting to all those victims of Christianity!

It is the religion! It is their priests, preachers, dogma and theories; it is even, sometimes, those simple, 'good', singing, brainwashed followers.

First of all: People created that Christian religion. And it has been serving fatefully, their desires and their urges. In the Christian religion, there is plenty of violence and injustice; it is all encoded. In fact, so much violence and injustice, that for millennia, each and every brutal ruler, cardinal, priest and crusader found enough 'inspiration' and 'justification' for his terrible deeds.

And the Empire is still feeding on that dogma and on the Bible, it keeps finding endless justifications and excuses for the terror that it is spreading all over the world. As all Christian Empires, for the last two thousand years, has been spreading fire and pain, reducing nations and people to pitiful slaves, and this planet, gradually, to… to what you know it is now!

As put brilliantly by G. W. Foote and J. M. Wheeler in their book "Crimes of Christianity": Both Catholic and Protestant have to face the fact that the triumph of Christianity was the triumph of barbarism, and that the doctrine of salvation by faith, is in each Church, the logical basis and sanction of persecution.

It is Christianity, the religion, not just the individuals. Christianity is guilty as charged!

***

I salute the men and women of the Middle East who fought the Crusaders.

I salute the African people, who did not allow themselves to be slaughtered and enslaved, shackled, and instead opted to die standing, than to live (or die anyway) on their knees.

I salute the revolutionaries of my beloved Latin America!

You kept our humanity alive. Thanks to you, I am still writing this essay! Thanks to you, countries like Venezuela and Cuba are standing, defiant and proud. Thanks to you, people all over the world are now waking up!

And I salute Christians, all over the world, who have realized that their religion is, always was and always will be, synonymous with crime, rape and plunder, even with countless genocides, and who have proudly divorced themselves from the Church and its 'heritage'!

This is my Easter salute! To the victims of Christian terror, and to those who have fought this the most fundamentalist, gloomy and destructive ideology on Earth, one that is closely associated with fascism, colonialism, racism and imperialism!

This is my Eastern celebration. Today I celebrate the lives of the heroes of the resistance against Christian terror!

And rest assured: "No one is forgotten, and nothing is forgotten!"

Andre Vltchek

9

UNITE AGAINST IMPERIALISM!

In countless interviews, in personal letters, in face-to-face discussions, the questions I keep being asked are becoming very similar: "Now that it is obvious that the West is ready and willing to destroy everything that stands in its way to the total domination of the planet, what can still be done?"

Some say: 'Nothing'. There are plenty of discouraged, scared voices of people who have already fully given up, and come to the conclusion that the Empire is too powerful, too determined, and therefore, unstoppable.

Others are praying. And there are also some, who are putting all their trust into those few brave ones that are 'still fighting'.

Hopelessness, fear and defeatism – this is how the Empire wants you to feel.

Do not! Defeat is only purposefully encoded in the propaganda that is being spread by the West. In reality, nothing is lost.

Actually, working all over the world, I am increasingly optimistic. People in the Middle East, in Africa, in many parts of Asia, are now waking up. People in Latin America woke up long time ago – they are alert, vigilant!

These are actually truly breathtaking moments in our human history. But nothing is free. To save the world, we will still have to stand firm against neo-colonialism, and all that insane propaganda that is being constantly disseminated by the West. We will have to be determined and strong. If we are, this is not going to be the end, but the beginning!

Of course if we just whine, everything will go to hell, and fall into the laps of the rulers of the world.

***

I actually think, and I have said it and written it on so many occasions, that right now there is absolutely no reason for nihilism.

Those dark days, some two decades ago, of disheartenment and gloom, are over. The era of the monsters like Reagan and Thatcher, the post-Reagan and post-Thatcher decades, of the Bush years, of the Yeltsin years, pre-Chavez years, pre-Morales years: Have all gone!

This is a new reality, and in many parts of the planet, it is quite a beautiful one!

Of course, most of the world is still extremely ugly, in pain and being governed by ruthless thugs, hypocrites, and even by mass murderers. Of course the West has not reformed itself, and it has never abandoned its ambition to dominate the planet. Of course there are millions of innocent people still dying, and the planet is being plundered by a bunch of degenerate morons belonging to the new religion called 'market fundamentalism'... as this is being written.

Of course the propaganda and brainwashing campaigns coming from North America and Europe are intensifying dangerously. Of course it is not 'the end of history', but 'the end of democracy' as we have always perceived it...

Democracy has been totally kidnapped, perverted and humiliated by the most cynical manipulations from Washington, London and Paris. It has nothing to do with the 'rule of the people', nor about sticking some piece of paper into a carton box, in order to legitimize an entirely illegitimate 'multi-party' (really multi-party?) regime.

And of course, if there is no determined resistance, or defense of the basic values on which humanity is based, there will soon be nothing except absolute slavery, market fundamentalism, in brief a society much more appalling than Orwell or Huxley could ever envision.

***

The good news is, that there is resistance!

And there are people who are standing tall and fighting for the survival of mankind.

But equally as important, or even more important, is the fact that now there are also several countries that are totally determined not to allow this neo-Nazi European and North American system to choke the world.

These countries are not 'perfect', as nothing on this earth is. But they are historically peaceful, even if dirtied by the relentless disinformation campaign carried out by the global mass media. And they are all, without exception, much more interested in the well-being of humankind, than in religious concepts attached to business doctrines or world domination.

These countries – they all have different histories, economic and political systems, but all of them are fundamentally against Western neo-colonialism and imperialism. Needless to say, all of them have suffered greatly from it in the past, so they know what they are fighting against.

I am talking about Cuba and Venezuela, Bolivia and Ecuador, Uruguay, China, Russia, Eritrea, Vietnam, Zimbabwe, Iran, and many other nations of our wonderful and diverse planet.

Each and every one of them has been attacked in the past, by either Europe or the United States, or both.

China, one of the oldest and greatest nations on earth, was tricked, occupied and divided; plundered... Barbaric French hordes ransacked its cultural treasures, while the British colonized its cities, and in fact entire areas.

Symbolically, as recorded, the invaders even looted Chinese cultural treasures. As written in 'The Telegraph': there are Chinese artifacts, "1.5 million artifacts... in museums and collections across Europe and America, including the British Museum and the Victoria & Albert Museum in London."

The West has been meddling in the internal affairs of China, financing, training and even arming its 'opposition'. The narrative over Tibet, as well as its mostly internationalist approach towards Africa (I have interviewed hundreds of African people on the ground, in twenty odd countries, and most of them were appalled by the Western anti-Chinese narrative), has been totally kidnapped by the propagandists in London and Washington. The country has been antagonized and provoked on various occasions, its neighbors pitched artificially against it, again and again.

The outrageous provocative military actions of the US, Japan and South Korea against China and North Korea, are continuously bringing the world somewhere close to WWIII, as I have been told by most of the leading academics specializing in the region, including many of those from the West. Europe or the United States would never tolerate even one percent of what they are subjecting China, Russia and other countries to, with deadly regularity.

Is there any rational, historical reason why the world should fear China or North Korea, or Vietnam? Of course not! Except that the world is constantly being bombarded by a 'religious' and impossible to prove demagogy, which describes China (not the West!), as the true aggressor.

The historical and present-day violence against Russia is even more extreme. In recent history, the West has openly attacked Russia, on countless occasions. To name just a few of the most deadly ones: WWI, as well as several incursions against the young Soviet State by the French, Czech and others. According to the BBC Russia Profile:

"In northern Russia, British, French and US troops

captured Murmansk and Archangel until 1919, while in the Russian Far East they occupied Vladivostok."

WWII terminated the lives of twenty million Soviet citizens, who in the end defeated Nazism and saved further hundreds of millions of people worldwide, from definite annihilation.

While the Soviet Union supported most of the liberation struggles in the fight against Western colonialism, it never directly attacked Western Europe nor the United States.

In the end, the Soviet Union was dragged into the Afghan conflict in 1979, and was financially and mentally exhausted, exactly in accordance with the plan created by Zbigniew Brzesinski. As I was recently told, in the city of Kharkov, by a Ukrainian political analyst, Alexandr Oleinik:

"The essence of what is now happening is based on the doctrine of the United States, which has one major goal: To wipe out from the globe, first the Soviet Union, and then Russia, regardless of its form; whether socialist or capitalist... As is well known, these goals were already defined in the early 1980s, by Zbigniew Brzezinski, in his report to the US State Department, titled: "Game Plan: A Geostrategic Framework for the Conduct of the U.S.-Soviet Contest."

But it is Russia, not the US, UK or France, which is constantly defined by Western propaganda as the aggressor! No facts are given, except for many pseudo-facts about the Ukrainian famine, which, this author is intending to re-visit from his previous essays, together with the other 'main pillars of Western anti-Communist propaganda' – the Chinese famine and Cambodian bloodletting (both triggered by imperialism – by the US and Japanese ones), but about these topics, a little bit later this year.

Could all these vicious lies and manipulations be created precisely because Russia has always fought against Western imperialism?

And what about the world? Just ask people from the Middle East, Latin America, and Africa: Many see both Russia and China as two giants, two heroes, not as 'aggressors'.

Iran: Is there any country (maybe except Cuba and Russia),

which has suffered from Western terror more than this old cultural powerhouse?

Iran has been battered relentlessly! The democratically elected Prime Minister Mohammad Mosaddegh, a true patriot who introduced great social changes in his country, was overthrown in a CIA and MI6 arranged coup, in 1953. It is not even denied in the West. The New York Times in 2000, reported ("The C.I.A. In Iran") on that fact, and called the operation a 'success', lamenting 'mishaps':

"The Central Intelligence Agency's secret history of its covert operation to overthrow Iran's government in 1953 offers an inside look at how the agency stumbled into success, despite a series of mishaps that derailed its original plans."

The West then pampered and supported its brutal implant, the Shah; his torture chambers, rapes, political murders and disappearances. And it armed and conditioned Iraq, which was under its close ally – Saddam Hussein – who invaded Iran in 1987, triggering a beastly war that took between 500,000 and 1.5 million human lives (historians can still not agree on the exact numbers).

Iran, naturally, has never attacked Europe or the United States, but we are told to fear its 'potential nuclear capability'! Of course it did something much more 'terrible' in the eyes of the West; it dared to, under Mosaddegh, to nationalize its oil reserves. For that, millions of people had to die.

I don't know about others, but while looking back at our planet's history, I'd feel calmer if Iran were to have nukes, than when I know for certain, that the UK, France or US, some of the most aggressive countries on earth, actually have them.

And Cuba! Assassination plots against its President, the bombing of a passenger airliner, the bombing of restaurants and hotels, a direct invasion, an insane embargo, and even attempts to trigger drought and poison its crops, not to speak about the direct financing of the 'dissidents'! The West, led mainly by the United States, did all that to Cuba. And it was done with absolute impunity.

All this because Cuba has been fighting, for decades, against imperialism and colonialism in Africa, because it helped to liberate Namibia and Angola, and tried to liberate the Congo; because it has been sending its doctors to the poorest parts of the world, because it has become a symbol of resistance against Western fascism...

Are we all scared of Cuba? Hands up who is! I am serious.

I can go on and on, about Venezuela and Bolivia, about Chile, even Brazil. But this time I just want to send a relatively short message: Just once, just for a few minutes, let us 'censor' our minds, to all the propaganda coming from the West. And let us, based on history and common sense, ask a very logical question: "Would it not be better to give a chance to those countries that are now standing against the Empire?"

We let Europe, the United States and their religious market fundamentalists rule the world, for many long centuries, and hundreds of millions of people vanished. Just let us have a glance at the map of the world, the way it looked at the very beginning of the 20th century. Are we getting the point? Everything colonized by Europe, all divided, messed up and enslaved.

Let us try something else. Let us all join the fight against Nazism and imperialism. Let us at least try!

***

Slowly but surely, non-Western countries are joining hands: Russia and Latin America, China and Latin America (yes, it was China which bailed out and saved Cuba, when that traitorous alcoholic Yeltsin, was busy destroying his country and the world, while at the same time taking direct Western dictates). Russia and China are getting closer, while Russia declared that it would support and defend Iran, if necessary. Venezuela and Iran, despite their cultural and social differences, are now as close as possible, and so are countries like Brazil and China.

The world is changing.

New and powerful media has emerged, sheltering the world from the one-sided Western indoctrination, offering great alternatives:

'TeleSur' in Venezuela (for which we are laboring relentlessly and proudly!). Press TV. RT! And there is even CCTV of China, although it still has to shed its 'shyness'.

All this new and potent media is being read watched and relied on, by tens of millions of people starved of honest reporting and anti-imperialist stands! These media outlets are now standing tall and firm, alongside those several great opposition publications in the West (mainly in North America, very little in Europe) such as Counterpunch, Global Research, and Znet.

***

Public disobedience and "Occupy Wall Street" will definitely not save the world.

Whole countries, big and strong, will have to get involved.

There should be no appeasement. If the Empire dares to put its destroyers and military bases near Russia, China, Iran or Venezuela, these countries should do the same. And they are doing it, and they will.

The West is increasingly acting as a Nazi entity, and one does not do 'peaceful protests' in front of the Reichstag, when flames are consuming the world, when millions are being murdered!

Such protests will only be tolerated for as long as they are ineffective, but the moment when they truly become dangerous to the empire, they will be crushed. As they were!

I also believe that internal opposition in Europe and the United States should stop being so picky, demanding purity and perfection from the countries that are fighting against their own Nazi rulers, the system and the Empire. It's not the time to be too fussy.

Resistance forces are diverse, they are not always ideal and to everyone's taste, but they are already saving millions of human lives.

Let us first stop Western aggressions, imperialism and neo-colonialism, and only then, let us sort out our differences and determine the ideological way forward for the progressive forces on this planet.

Until then, to the barricades, to the battleships and to the television stations and magazines!

Of course we will win, but it will take some balls and ovaries, as they say in Latin America!

Andre Vltchek

10

DOWN WITH WESTERN 'DEMOCRACY'

A specter is haunting Europe and Western world — it is this time, the specter of fascism. It came quietly, without great fanfare and parades, without raised hands and loud shouts. But it came, or it returned, as it has always been present in this culture, one that has, for centuries, been enslaving our entire planet.

As was in Nazi Germany, resistance to the fascist empire is again given an unsavory name: terrorism. Partisans and patriots, resistance fighters – all of them were and have always been defined by fascist bigots as terrorists.

By the logic of Empire, to murder millions of men, women and children in all corners of the world abroad is considered legitimate and patriotic, but to defend one's motherland was and is a sign of extremism.

German Nazis and Italian Fascists defined their rule as 'democratic', and so does this Empire. The British and French empires that exterminated tens of millions of people all over the world, always promoted themselves as 'democracies'.

And now, once again, we are witnessing a tremendous

onslaught by the business-political-imperialist Western apparatus, destabilizing or directly destroying entire nations, overthrowing governments and bombing 'rebellious' states into the ground.

All this is done in the name of democracy, in the name of freedom.

An unelected monster, as it has done for centuries, is playing with the world, torturing some, and plundering others, or both.

The West, in a final act of arrogance, has somehow confused itself with its own concept of God. It has decided that it has the full right to shape the planet, to punish and to reward, to destroy and rebuild as it wishes.

This horrible wave of terror unleashed against our planet, is justified by an increasingly meaningless but fanatically defended dogma, symbolized by a box (made of card or wood, usually), and masses of people sticking pieces of paper into the opening on the top of that box.

This is the altar of Western ideological fundamentalism. This is a supreme idiocy that cannot be questioned, as it guarantees the status quo for ruling elites and business interests, an absurdity that justifies all crimes, all lies and all madness.

This sacrificial altar is called, Democracy, in direct mockery to what the term symbolizes in its original, Greek, language.

***

In our latest book, "On Western Terrorism – from Hiroshima to Drone Warfare", Noam Chomsky commented on the 'democratic' process in the Western world:

"The goal of elections now is to undermine democracy. They are run by the public relations industry and they're certainly not trying to create informed voters who'll make rational choices. They are trying to delude people into making irrational choices. The same techniques that are used to undermine markets are used to undermine democracy. It's one of the major industries in the country and its basic workings are invisible."

But what is it that really signifies this 'sacred' word, this almost religious term, and this pinnacle of Western demagogy? We hear it everywhere. We are ready to sacrifice millions of lives (not ours of course, at least not yet, but definitely lives of the others) in the name of it.

Democracy!

All those grand slogans and propaganda! Last year I visited Pyongyang, but I have to testify that North Koreans are not as good at slogans as the Western propagandists are.

"In the name of freedom and democracy!" Hundreds of millions tons of bombs fell from the sky on the Laotian, Cambodian and Vietnamese countryside... bodies were burned by napalm, mutilated by spectacular explosions.

"Defending democracy!" Children were raped in front of their parents in Central America, men and women machine-gunned down by death squads that had been trained in military bases in the United States of America.

"Civilizing the world and spreading democracy!" That has always been a European slogan, their 'stuff to do', and a way of showing their great civilization to others. Amputating hands of Congolese people, murdering around ten million of them, and many more in Namibia, East Africa, West Africa and Algiers; gassing people of the Middle East ("I am strongly in favour of using poisonous gas against uncivilised tribes", to borrow from the colorful lexicon of (Sir) Winston Churchill).

So what is it really? Who is it, that strange lady with an axe in her hand and with a covered face – the lady whose name is Democracy?

***

It is all very simple, actually. The term originates from the Greek δημοκρατία (dēmokratía) "rule of the people". Then and now, it was supposed to be in direct contrast to ἀριστοκρατία (aristokratia), that means "rule of an elite".

'Rule of the people'... Let us just visit a few examples of the 'rule of the people'.

People spoke, they ruled, they voted 'democratically' in Chile, bringing in the mild and socialist government of 'Popular Unity' of Salvador Allende.

Sure, the Chilean education system was so brilliant, its political and social system so wonderful, that it inspired not only many countries in Latin America, but also those in far away Mediterranean Europe.

That could not be tolerated, because, as we all know, it is only white Europe and North America that can be allowed to supply the world with the blueprint for any society, anywhere on this planet. It was decided that "Chile has to scream", that its economy had to be ruined and the "Popular Unity" government kicked out of power.

Henry Kissinger, belonging, obviously, to a much higher race and country of a much higher grade, made a straightforward and in a way very 'honest' statement, clearly defining the North American stand towards global democracy: "I don't see why we need to stand by and watch a country go Communist due to the irresponsibility of its people."

And so Chile was ravaged. Thousands of people were murdered and 'our son-of-a-bitch' was brought to power. General Pinochet was not elected: he bombed the Presidential palace in Santiago, he savagely tortured the men and women who were elected by the Chilean people, and he "disappeared" thousands.

But that was fine, because democracy, as it is seen from Washington, London or Paris, is nothing more and nothing less than what the white man needs in order to control this planet, unopposed and preferably never criticized.

Of course Chile was not the only place where 'democracy' was 'redefined'. And it was not the most brutal scenario either, although it was brutal enough. But it was a very symbolic 'case', because here, there could be absolutely no dispute: an extremely well educated, middle class country, voted in transparent elections, just to have its government murdered, tortured and exiled, simply because it was too democratic and too involved in improving the lives of its people.

There were countless instances of open spite coming from the North, towards the 'rule of the people' in Latin America. For centuries, there have been limitless examples. Every country 'south of the border' in the Western Hemisphere, became a victim.

After all, the self-imposed Monroe Doctrine gave North Americans 'unquestionable rights' to intervene and 'correct' any 'irresponsible' democratic moves made by the lower races inhabiting Central and South America as well as the Caribbean Islands.

There were many different scenarios of real ingenuity, in how to torture countries that embarked on building decent homes for their people, although soon there was evidence of repetitiveness and predictability.

The US has been either sponsoring extremely brutal coups (like the one in Guatemala in 1954), or simply occupying the countries in order to overthrow their democratically elected governments. Justifications for such interventions have varied: it was done in order to 'restore order', to 'restore freedom and democracy', or to prevent the emergence of 'another Cuba'.

From the Dominican Republic in 1965 to Grenada in 1983, countries were 'saved from themselves' through the introduction (by orders from mainly the Protestant North American elites with clearly pathological superiority complexes) of death squads that administered torture, rape and extrajudicial executions. People were killed because their democratic decisions were seen as 'irresponsible' and therefore unacceptable.

While there has been open racism in every aspect of how the Empire controlled its colonies, 'political correctness' was skillfully introduced, effectively reducing to a bare minimum any serious critiques of the societies that were forced into submission.

In Indonesia, between 1 and 3 million people were murdered in the years1965/66, in a US -sponsored coup, because there too, was a 'great danger' that the people would rule and decide to vote 'irresponsibly', bringing the Communist Party of Indonesia (PKI), at that time the third most numerous Communist Party anywhere in the world, to power.

The democratically elected President of Congo, Patrice Lumumba, was murdered in 1961, by the joint efforts of the United States and Europe, simply because he was determined to use the vast natural resources of his country to feed his own people; and because he dared to criticize Western colonialism and imperialism openly and passionately.

East Timor lost a third of its population simply because its people, after gaining independence from Portugal, dared to vote the left-leaning FRETILIN into power. "We are not going to tolerate another Cuba next to our shores", protested the Indonesian fascist dictator Suharto, and the US and Australia strongly agreed. The torture, and extermination of East Timorese people by the Indonesian military, was considered irrelevant and not even worth reporting in the mass media.

The people of Iran could of course not be trusted with 'democracy'. Iran is one of the oldest and greatest cultures on earth, but its people wanted to use the revenues from its oil to improve their lives, not to feed foreign multi-nationals. That has always been considered a crime by Western powers – a crime punishable by death.

The people of Iran decided to rule; they voted, they said that they want to have all their oil industry nationalized. Mohammad Mosaddeq, the democratically elected Prime Minister of Iran from 1951 to 1953, was ready to implement what his people demanded. But his government was overthrown in a coup d'état, orchestrated by the British MI6 and North American CIA, and what followed was the murderous dictatorship of the deranged Western puppet – Reza Pahlavi. As in Latin America and Indonesia, instead of schools, hospitals and housing projects, people got death squads, torture chambers and fear. Is that what they wanted? Is that what they voted for?

There were literally dozens of countries, all over the world, which had to be 'saved', by the West, from their own 'irresponsible citizens and voters'. Brazil recently 'celebrated' the 50th anniversary of the US-backed military coup d'état, which began a horrendous 20 year long military dictatorship. The US supported two coups in Iraq, in 1963 and 1968 that brought Saddam Hussein and his Baath Party to power. The list is endless. These are only some random examples.

On closer examination, the West has overthrown, or made attempts to overthrow, almost any democratically elected governments, on all continents attempting to serve their own people, by providing them with decent standards of living and social services. That is quite an achievement, and some stamina!

Could it be then that the West only respects 'Democracy' when 'people are forced to rule' against their own interests? And when they are 'defending' what they are ordered to defend by local elites that are subservient to North American and European interests?... and also when they are defending the interests of foreign multi-national companies and Western governments that are dependent on those companies?

***

Can anything be done? If a country is too weak to defend itself by military means, against some mighty Western aggressor, could it approach any international democratic institutions, hoping for protection?

Unthinkable!

A good example is Nicaragua, which had been literally terrorized by the United States, for no other reason than for being socialist. Its government went to court.

The case was called: The Republic of Nicaragua v. The United States of America.

It was a 1986 case at the International Court of Justice (ICJ) in which the ICJ ruled in favor of Nicaragua and against the United States and awarded reparations to Nicaragua.

The judgment was long, consisting of 291 points. Among

them that the United States had been involved in the "unlawful use of force." The alleged violations included attacks on Nicaraguan facilities and naval vessels, the mining of Nicaraguan ports, the invasion of Nicaraguan air space, and the training, arming, equipping, financing and supplying of forces (the "Contras") and seeking to overthrow Nicaragua's Sandinista government.

Judgment was passed, and so were UN votes and resolutions. The UN resolution from 1986 called for the full and immediate compliance with the Judgment. Only Thailand, France and the UK abstained. The US showed total spite towards the court, and it vetoed all UN resolutions.

It continued its terror campaign against Nicaragua. In the end, the ruined and exhausted country voted in 1990. It was soon clear that it was not voting for or against Sandinista government, but whether to endure more violence from the North, or to simply accept depressing defeat. The Sandinista government lost. It lost because the voters had a North American gun pointing at their heads.

This is how 'democracy' works.

I covered the Nicaraguan elections of 1996 and I was told by voters, by a great majority of them, that they were going to vote for the right-wing candidate (Aleman), only because the US was threatening to unleash another wave of terror in case the Sandinista government came back to power, democratically.

The Sandinistas are now back. But only because most of Latin America has changed, and there is unity and determination to fight, if necessary.

***

While the Europeans are clearly benefiting from neo-colonialism and the plunder that goes on all over the world, it would be ridiculous to claim that they themselves are 'enjoying the fruits of democracy'.

In a dazzling novel "Seeing", written by Jose Saramago, a

laureate for the Nobel Prize for literature, some 83% of voters in an unidentified country (most likely Saramago's native Portugal), decide to cast blank ballots, expressing clear spite towards the Western representative election system.

This state, which prided itself as a 'democratic one', responded by unleashing an orgy of terror against its own citizens. It soon became obvious that people are allowed to make democratic choices only when the result serves the interests of the regime.

Ursula K Le Guin, reviewing the novel in the pages of The Guardian, on 15 April 2006, admitted:

Turning in a blank ballot is a signal unfamiliar to most Britons and Americans, who aren't yet used to living under a government that has made voting meaningless. In a functioning democracy, one can consider not voting a lazy protest liable to play into the hands of the party in power (as when low Labour turn-out allowed Margaret Thatcher's re-elections, and Democratic apathy secured both elections of George W Bush). It comes hard to me to admit that a vote is not in itself an act of power, and I was at first blind to the point Saramago's non-voting voters are making.

She should not have been. Even in Europe itself, terror had been unleashed, on many occasions, against the people who decided to vote 'incorrectly'.

Perhaps the most brutal instance was in the post WWII period, when the Communist Parties were clearly heading for spectacular victories in France, Italy and West Germany. Such 'irresponsible behavior' had to be, of course, stopped. Both US and UK intelligence forces made a tremendous effort to 'save democracy' in Europe, employing Nazis to break, intimidate, even murder members of progressive movements and parties.

These Nazi cadres were later allowed, even encouraged, to leave Europe for South America, some carrying huge booty from the victims who vanished in concentration camps. This booty included gold teeth.

Later on, in the 1990's, I spoke to some of them, and also to their children, in Asuncion, the capital of Paraguay. They were proud of their deeds, unrepentant, and as Nazi as ever.

Many of those European Nazis later actively participated in Operation Condor, so enthusiastically supported by the Paraguayan fascist and pro-Western dictator, Alfredo Strössner. Mr Strössner was a dear friend and asylum-giver to many WWII war criminals, including people like Dr. Josef Mengele, the Nazi doctor known as the "Angel of Death", who performed genetic experiments on children during the WWII.

So, after destroying that 'irresponsible democratic process' in Europe (the post-war Western Empire), many European Nazis that were now loyally serving their new master, were asked to continue with what they knew how to do best. Therefore they helped to assassinate some 60,000 left-wing South American men, women and their children, who were guilty of building egalitarian and just societies in their home countries. Many of these Nazis took part, directly, in Operacion Condor, under the direct supervision of the United States and Europe.

As Naomi Klein writes in her book, Shock Doctrine:

"Operación Cóndor, also known as Plan Cóndor, Portuguese: Operação Condor) was a campaign of political repression and terror involving intelligence operations and assassination of opponents, officially implemented in 1975 by the right-wing dictatorships of the Southern Cone of South America. The program was intended to eradicate communist or Soviet influence and ideas, and to suppress active or potential opposition movements against the participating governments."

In Chile, German Nazis rolled up their sleeves and went to work directly: by interrogating, liquidating and savagely torturing members of the democratically elected government and its supporters. They also performed countless medical experiments on people, at the so-called Colonia Dirnidad, during the dictatorship of Augusto Pinochet, whose rule was manufactured and sustained by Dr. Kissinger and his clique.

But back to Europe: in Greece, after WWII, both the UK and US got heavily involved in the civil war between the

Communists and the extreme right-wing forces.

In 1967, just one month before the elections in which the Greek left-wing was expected to win democratically (the Indonesian scenario of 1965), the US and its 'Greek colonels' staged a coup, which marked the beginning of a 7 year savage dictatorship.

What happened in Yugoslavia, some 30 years later is, of course clear. A successful Communist country could not be allowed to survive, and definitely not in Europe. As bombs fell on Belgrade, many of those inquisitive and critically thinking people that had any illusions left about the Western regime and its 'democratic principles', lost them rapidly.

But by then, the majority of Europe already consisted of indoctrinated masses, some of the worst informed and most monolithic (in their thinking) on earth.

Europe and its voters... It is that constantly complaining multitude, which wants more and more money, and delivers the same and extremely predictable electoral results every four, five or six years. It lives and votes mechanically. It has totally lost its ability to imagine a different world, to fight for humanist principles, and even to dream.

It is turning into an extremely scary place, a museum at best, and a cemetery of human vision at the worst.

**

As Noam Chomsky pointed out:

Americans may be encouraged to vote, but not to participate more meaningfully in the political arena. Essentially the election is a method of marginalizing the population. A huge propaganda campaign is mounted to get people to focus on these personalized quadrennial extravaganzas and to think, "That's politics." But it isn't. It's only a small part of politics.

The population has been carefully excluded from political activity, and not by accident. An enormous amount of work has gone into that disenfranchisement. During the 1960s the outburst of popular participation in democracy terrified the forces of convention, which mounted a fierce counter-campaign. Manifestations show up today on the left as well as the right in the effort to drive democracy back into the hole where it belongs.

Arundhati Roy, commented in her "Is there life after democracy?"

The question here, really, is what have we done to democracy? What have we turned it into? What happens once democracy has been used up? When it has been hollowed out and emptied of meaning? What happens when each of its institutions has metastasized into something dangerous? What happens now that democracy and the Free Market have fused into a single predatory organism with a thin, constricted imagination that revolves almost entirely around the idea of maximizing profit? Is it possible to reverse this process? Can something that has mutated go back to being what it used to be?

***

After all that brutality, and spite for people all over the world, the West is now teaching the planet about democracy. It is lecturing Asians and Africans, people from Middle East and Sub-Continent, on how to make their countries more 'democratic'. It is actually hard to believe, it should be one of the most hilarious things on earth, but it is happening, and everyone is silent about it.

Those who are listening without bursting into laughter are actually well paid.

There are seminars; even foreign aid projects related to 'good governance', sponsored by the European Union, and the United States. The EU is actually much more active in this field. Like the Italian mafia, it sends covert but unmistakable messages to the world: "You do as we say, or we break your legs... But if you obey, come to us and we will teach you how to be a good aide to Cosa Nostra! And we will give you some pasta and wine while you are learning."

Because there is plenty of money, so called 'funding'... members of the elite, the academia, media and non-government organizations, from countries that have been plundered by the West – countries like Indonesia, Philippines, DR Congo, Honduras, or Colombia –send armies of people to get voluntarily indoctrinated, (sorry, to be 'enlightened') to learn about democracy from the greatest assassins of genuine 'people's power'; from the West.

Violating democracy is an enormous business. To hush it up is part of that business. To learn how to be idle and not to intervene against the external forces destroying democracy in your own country, while pretending to be 'engaged and active', is actually the best business, much better than building bridges or educating children (from a mercantilist point of view).

Once, at the University of Indonesia where I was invited to speak, a student asked me 'what is the way forward', to make his country more democratic? I replied, looking at several members of the professorial staff:

"Demand that your teachers stop going to Europe on fully funded trips. Demand that they stop being trained in how to brainwash you. Do not go there yourself, to study. Go there to see, to understand and to learn, but not to study... Europe had robbed you of everything. They are still looting your country. What do you think you will learn there? Do you really think they will teach you how to save your nation?"

Students began laughing. The professors were fuming. I was never invited back. I am sure that the professors knew exactly what I was talking about. The students did not. They were thinking that I made a very good joke. But I was not trying to be funny.

***

As I write these words, the Thai military junta has taken over the country. The West is silent: the Thai military is an extremely close ally. Democracy at work...

And as I write these words, the fascist government in Kiev

131

is chasing, kidnapping and "disappearing" people in the east and south of Ukraine. By some insane twist of logic, the Western corporate media is managing to blame Russia. And only a few people are rolling around on the floor, laughing.

As I write these words, a big part of Africa is in flames, totally destroyed by the US, UK, France and other colonial powers.

Client states like the Philippines are now literally being paid to get antagonistic with China.

Japanese neo-fascist adventurism fully supported by the Unites States can easily trigger WWIII. So can Western greed and fascist practices in Ukraine.

Democracy! People's power!

If the West had sat on its ass, where it belongs, in Europe and in North America, after WWII, the world would have hardly any problems now. People like Lumumba, Allende, Sukarno, Mosaddeq, would have led their nations and continents. They would have communicated with their own people, interacted with them. They would have built their own styles of 'democracy'.

But all that came from the Bandung Conference of 1955, from the ideals of the Non-Aligned movement, was ruined and bathed in blood. The true hopes of the people of the world cut to pieces, urinated on, and then thrown into gutter.

But no more time should be wasted by just analyzing, and by crying over spilt milk. Time to move on!

The world has been tortured by Europe and the United States, for decades and centuries. It has been tortured in the name of democracy... but it has all been one great lie. The world has been tortured simply because of greed, and because of racism. Just look back at history. Europe and the United States have only stopped calling people "niggers", but they do not have any more respect for them than before. And they are willing, same as before, to sacrifice millions of human lives.

Let us stop worshiping their box, and those meaningless pieces of paper that they want us to stick in there. There is no power of people in this. Look at the United States itself – where is our democracy? It is a one-party regime fully controlled by market fundamentalists. Look at our press, and propaganda...

Rule of the people by the people, true democracy, can be achieved. We the people had been derailed, intellectually, so we have not been thinking how, for so many decades.

Now we, many of us, know what is wrong, but we are still not sure what is right.

Let us think and let us search, let us experiment. And also, let us reject their fascism first. Let them stick their papers wherever they want! Let them pretend that they are not slaves to some vendors and swindlers. Let them do whatever they want – there, where they belong.

Democracy is more than a box. It is more than a multitude of political parties. It is when people can truly choose, decide and build a society that they dream about. Democracy is the lack of fear of having napalm and bombs murdering our dreams. Democracy is when people speak and from those words grow their own nation. Democracy is when millions of hands join together and from that brilliant union, new trains begin to run, new schools begin to teach, and new hospitals begin to heal. All this by the people, for the people! All this created by proud and free humans as gift to all – to their nation.

Yes, let the slave masters stick their pieces of paper into a box, or somewhere else. They can call it democracy. Let us call democracy something else – rule of the people, a great exchange of ideas, of hopes and dreams. Let our taking control over our lives and over our nations be called 'democracy'!

ABOUT THE AUTHOR

Novelist, filmmaker, investigative journalist, poet, playwright, and photographer, Andre has covered dozens of war zones and conflicts from Bosnia and Peru to Sri Lanka, DR Congo and Timor Leste.

He is the author of a novel *Nalezeny*, published in Czech. *Point of No Return* is his major work of fiction written in English and translated and published in French by Edition Yago. Other works include a book of political nonfiction *Western Terror: From Potosi to Baghdad* (translated into Turkish and published by Bilim + Gonul). Pluto publishing house in London recently published his provocative and critical book *Indonesia: Archipelago of Fear.* Together with Rossie Indira, he is responsible for a book of conversations with the foremost Southeast Asian writer Pramoedya Ananta Toer, *Exile* (translated into Korean, Spanish and Bahasa Indonesia). Non-fiction book *Oceania* is a result of his five years work in Micronesia, Polynesia and Melanesia and a damning attack against neo-colonialism in the Pacific. His latest book *On Western Terrorism* is written with Noam Chomsky.

The plays *Ghosts of Valparaiso* and *Conversations with James* were translated into several languages including Spanish.

He has collaborated with UNESCO in Vietnam, Africa and Oceania through various publications including fiction books *The Story of Ann* and *The Story of Moana*. Presently he is finishing writing his monumental political novel *Winter Journey*.

He is a Senior Fellow at The Oakland Institute.

He writes and photographs for several publications worldwide, corporate and progressive, including RT, CounterPunch, Z Magazine, Newsweek, Asia Times, People's Daily, China Daily, Irish Times, A2 and Asia-Pacific Journal (Japan Focus).

He produced the feature length documentary film about the Indonesian massacres in 1965 *'Terlena – Breaking of The Nation'*, as well as the film on the biggest refugee camp in the world Dadaab *'One Flew Over Dadaab'*. His feature documentary film *'Rwandan Gambit'* is reversing the official narrative on 1994, exposing Rwandan and Ugandan plunder of DR Congo on behalf of Western imperialism. His Japanese crew recently filmed his lengthy debate with Noam Chomsky on the state of the world which is presently being made into a film. He produced several documentaries for South American TV Network TeleSur. He is working on several new documentaries in Asia, Africa, and Latin America.

He frequently speaks at major universities, including Columbia, Cornell, Oxford, Cambridge, Sydney, Hong Kong, Auckland and Melbourne. Cofounder and Coeditor of Mainstay Press and Liberation Lit, he presently lives in Asia and Africa. His website is: http://andrevltchek.weebly.com/index.html. And his twitter is: @AndreVltchek.

Compliments for Andre Vltchek:

"Andre Vltchek tells us about a world that few know, even when they think they do. That is because he tells the truth, vividly, with a keen sense of history, and with a perceptive eye that sees past surfaces to reality..." *Noam Chomsky*

"Vltchek has written a colorful and elegantly crafted novel with a political stance that will engage some and provoke others but is always heart-felt and sincere." *Lila Rajiva*

"André Vltchek is a writer, the real thing, of the same calibre and breed as Hemingway and Malraux." *Catherine Merveilleux (Marseille)*

"André Vltchek offers an unsparing portrait of the world we live in. With his provocative outlook, he lays bare a situation that is really quite simple, and did not begin yesterday: a small group of nations whose economic system has nothing to do with humanism, solidarity or compassion, governs the world, exploiting the poorest countries, making a mockery along the way of the democratic principles humanity has been struggling to uphold for centuries. He also recounts the innumerable excesses that accrue as a result, and touches on the subject of religion, which teaches submission." *Françoise Bachelet*

"A serious piece of writing endowed with great sincerity, portraying a unique life experience that leaves us feeling forlorn even as it pulls us along in its wake." *Nathalie Zylberman*

"Once again, it's the context that makes the book. It is quite simply mind-boggling. Andre Vltchek knows very well what he's talking about..." *Yves Mabon*

"Reading this book prompts certain reflections: to what degree can one be a witness and remain uninvolved, without being responsible? (...) An instructive and brilliant book that forces the reader to face the question: What sort of world are we leaving to our children? How could we ever justify ourselves? How far are we willing to go to change it?" *Valérie Revelut*

CPSIA information can be obtained
at www.ICGtesting.com
Printed in the USA
FFOW02n2210171115
18764FF